Contemporary Gospel Accents

Doing Theology in Africa, Asia, Southeast Asia, and Latin America

Contemporary Gospel Accents

Doing Theology in Africa, Asia, Southeast Asia, and Latin America

EDITED BY DANIEL CARRO AND RICHARD F. WILSON

MERCER UNIVERSITY PRESS • MACON, GEORGIA • 1997

CONTEMPORARY GOSPEL ACCENTS

Contempoary Gospel Accents: doing theology in Africa, Asia, Southeast Asia,
    and Latin America / edited by Daniel Carro and Richard F. Wilson.
    p.   cm.
Papers presented at a Baptist World Alliance Seminar held in August 1995 in
    Buenos Aires, Argentina.
    Includes bibliographical references.
    ISBN 0-86554-505-7
    1. Baptists—Developing countries—Doctrines—History—20th century—
Congresses. 2. Christianity and culture—Developing countries—History of
doctrines—20th century—Congresses.
I. Carro, Daniel. II. Wilson, Richard Francis, 1953–. III. Baptist World
Alliance.
Bx6331,2,C67 1996
230'.6'09—dc20
                                                                96–32798
                                                                    CIP

The paper used in this publication meets the minimum requirements of
American National Standard for Information Services—Permanance of Paper for
Printed Library materials,
ANSI Z39.48-1984.

Printed in the United States of America.

Table of Contents

Preface

"porque tengo el corazón mirando al sur"
("because I have my heart facing toward the South")

A certain Argentine *tango*[1] concludes with the above words, suggesting that the direction one faces is more a matter of the heart than of the mind. The leanings of the heart do shape the leanings of the mind. The essays and confessions found in the following pages are "facing toward the South" because they were forged in hearts and minds that call the South—south of the equator, that is—home.[2] At the close of the twentieth century the accents of theologians from the South need to be heard. For too long the accents from the North and West have dominated theological confession. Contemporary gospel accents have a southern form, too.

That our world has always been divided into irreconcilable parties is true, but it does not mean that is the way our world should remain. From the beginnings of the Christian faith the greatest challenge of the church has been to live toward the sort of integration that breaks down the walls of separation that keep sisters and brothers from benefitting from one another's insights and compassion. Unfortunately Christians in the church have failed more often than we have succeeded in living in the kind of global community the gospel promises.

Throughout history Christianity has been predisposed to accentuate extremes of differences rather than ameliorate the tendencies toward division. *Sola fide* has not been a friend of good works. Evangelism does not seem to sympathize with social action. Ethical demands seem contrary to the spiritual impulses of prayer and worship. More graphic are the myriad divisions that impose themselves on our global community—Jew–Gentile, male–female, slave–free, East–West, white–black—these are the polarities into which we have divided the one Body of Christ. And we must add the polarity of North–South.

The exclusivistic perspectives that plague Christianity also have divided us among ourselves. The rifts between Protestants and Catholics run deep around the world, as do the chasms that separate sisters and brothers within the same historic families of faith, including the Baptist family. As each group attempts to retreat into a home more narrow than the gospel allows, more and more divisions emerge, giving rise to innumerable sects, cults, churches, communities, denominations and the like that have been born from our narrow interpretations.

The last quarter of the twentieth century is issuing a cry for unification, or so it seems. The fall of the Berlin Wall in 1989, and the subsequent rapid thaw of the Cold War that had kept the globe frozen in pockets of particularity is a great example of a hope for unity and reunion. A globalization of culture and a new world order now appear as the likely paths toward the future.

The beginnings of globalization in our world holds promise for the day when there no longer will be East or West, and no North or South. The one division in our world that remains—and is growing at an alarming rate—is the division between the rich and the poor. The wealthy grow more so every day while the impoverished sink deeper and deeper into the mire of want and need.

The growing urbanization in Latin America is a good illustration. Right now three out of four Latin Americans live in cities; by the year 2000 the ratio is expected to be five out of six Latin Americans identified as urban dwellers. Add to urbanization the demographic explosion: more than 50% of the population in Mexico City are younger than 16, for example. Factor in the acceleration of mass and personal communications, best represented by the World Wide Web (is it divine or demonic?), and an image of a frightening "global village" comes into focus. The world, it seems, is getting smaller and smaller. There is a saying in Spanish: *"pueblo chico, infierno grande"* ("small village, big hell"). The more the global village becomes a reality, the more our world resembles a big inferno.

Globalization carries with it an accentuation of power and wealth, as reflected in the popular slogan of capitalism: "Much more for many more." The ecomonic and political reality in regions of

South—south of the equator, that is—include unequal distribution of common goods, which in turn foster more poverty, more social injustice, more underemployment, more hunger, more disease, more illiteracy. Emphases on power and wealth also lead to the erosion of social and cultural values, the disintegration of society, and corruption as a way of life.

In the midst of the clamoring for globalization there is a profound need for a deliberate contextualization of our faith. A contextual faith is a desperate need all over the world. Although it once was assumed that the gospel could be interpreted one way in all places of the world, such is no longer the case. Reflecting the parable of the soils (Mark 4 and parallels), the time has come to allow the seed of the gospel to fall on diverse soils and come to maturity in ways that are appropriate to the soil—the region of the world—where it takes root. A contextualization of the gospel also calls for a contextualization of theology.

In 1993, when Baptist theological educators of the world met in Johannesburg, South Africa for the fourth Baptist International Conference on Theological Education (BICTE IV) to explore the demands of contextual theology, it seemed proper that theologians from the South—south of the equator, that is—engage one another. From these discussion groups an idea came forward: to meet formally and publicly in Buenos Aires, Argentina during the Baptist World Congress in 1995. Plans for a first-ever conference among Baptists interested in exploring contextual theology went into motion.

Convening the conference fell to the responsibility of a small committee who, under the direction of Wiard Popkes, Chairperson of the Academic and Theological Workgroup, and Tony Cupit, Director of Evangelism and Education and Study and Research of the Baptist World Alliance, invited a diverse group of Baptist theologians from around the world to write and present essays. For the purposes of the conference, the world was divided into four "southern" zones: Africa, Asia, Southeast Asia, and Latin America. The classification is obviously inadequate, but at least helped conveners to be fair in the distribution of papers.

When the conference began in Buenos Aires, Daniel Carro, a member of the planning committee, reported that Wiard Popkes had returned to Germany because of the death of his brother. Carro was then the moderator of the two-day conference. As well, some of the invited presenters were unable to make the trip. Those who sent their essays had their work read and discussed among a group of forty or so attendees. The same pattern was followed for papers read by those who wrote them. The result was a first step toward formal and public conversation among Baptist theologians about contextual theology.

Following the conference some additional papers were submitted. The essays and confessions that follow represent a compilation of papers written for the conference, most of which were delivered and discussed. The tasks of editing and arranging the papers were shared by Carro and Richard F. Wilson, a member of the Academic and Theological Workgroup.

Bringing an ambitious project to maturity required the work of many people around the world. The presenters and authors gave of themselves with candor and passion. Wiard Popkes and Tony Cupit performed the arduous tasks of planning. The conference was held in the chapel at the *Seminario Internacional Teológico Bautista*; faculty and staff provided a warm environment for the discussions.

All but one presenter prepared manuscripts in English, which was also the common language of the conference. Carlos Villanueva opted to write and deliver his paper in Spanish. Non-Spanish speakers were grateful for Stanley Clark, Jr. who served as an interpreter for Villanueva. English readers will be especially thankful for the fine translation prepared by Bob Adams, former professor at the *Seminario Internacional Teológico Bautista*, where he and Carlos were colleagues. Adams is a professor of Ethics and Missions at the Gardner-Webb University School of Divinity in Boiling Springs, North Carolina.

Mercer University Press agreed to publish the proceedings of the conference. Cecil Staton, publisher for MUP, is a fierce champion for Baptist heritage and we thank him for his support. R. Scott Nash began the publishing project with us and offered good insights and suggestions ranging from choosing a title to editorial advice to make the finished project as consistent as possible. Vaughn CroweTipton has watched over the final stages of publication.

Nancy Stubbs is the secretary for The Roberts Department of Christianity at Mercer University. She transferred all the typed manuscripts presenters provided to disk, making possible the work of the editors. We thank her for her good work and support. Finally, we owe a debt to Teresa Martin, Assistant in the Evangelism and Education Department of the Baptist World Alliance office in McLean, Virginia. Without her aid we never would have been able to include the proper titles and positions of all the contributors to this project.

There is a southern vision of the world; and there is a theology of the South—south of the equator, that is. The accents of its over-tones are emerging in this book. This book is a challenge and a call. It is a plea to those with a northern vision of the world to open them-selves to dialogue, and it is an invitation to our northern friends to enter a conversation about our views of the world, our faith in Christ, and the mission of the church today.

This book is the first word with an accent from the South—south of the equator, that is. The next word needs to fall from other lips and other pens, in other accents. Without the next word there will be no dialogue. Conversations only exist and grow with replies. Speak. We will listen.

Daniel Carro
Seminario Internacional
Teológico Bautista
Buenos Aires
Argentina

Richard F. Wilson
Mercer University
Macon, Georgia
United States

NOTES

[1]Most North American and European readers exclusively understand the *tango* as a form of dance that originated in Argentina. In fact, *tango* is a broader genre that includes sad ballads and songs of love. There is some affinity between the tone and style of "the blues" found throughout the southern states of the United States and the *tangos* of Argentina.

[2]The notable exception is the essay by Eddie Kin-ming Ma who writes as theologian from Hong Kong in the face of reabsorption by China. Even then, however, the image of having a heart facing toward the South is apt, since Hong Kong is in the lengthening shadows of China to the North.

Foreword

L.A. (Tony) Cupit

Fresh, compelling voices from theologians of the southern hemisphere should challenge us all to sit up and listen. If the dynamic impulse in mission and evangelism in our age is coming from the developing world; if issues of justice and peace are having their strongest expression from the same areas; if churches are growing fastest in Latin American, Africa and Asia; then choosing not to listen to theologians and theological educators from these regions would indeed be foolish.

As the director of the evangelism and education concerns for the Baptist World Alliance, I have the privilege of visiting Baptist theological schools all over the world. The way Baptists conduct theological and ministerial training in places where resources are often limited, buildings sub-standard and library facilities totally inadequate is inspiring.

The testimonies of eager students in states of India, such as Assam, Meghalaya and Nagaland, Bangladesh, and similar testimonies in the highlands of Papua New Guinea, in Cuba, and in Zambia are thrilling. Through them I have begun to understand that despite almost insurmountable obstacles, Baptists are teaching and learning the great truths from the Word of God. The teaching and learning find room in valleys, on hills, in cities and hamlets—where ever a Baptist body forms.

Some Baptist theological institutions are located in very modern, progressive cities where technology is advanced, the faculty highly educated, and the facilities outstanding. Some schools, by contrast, are found in jungle clearings, where floors are dirt, walls are bamboo, and the roofs are woven from grass. One or two embattled educators bear huge teaching loads, and they have little opportunity to upgrade their

Contemporary Gospel Accents

formal qualifications as teachers. Nonetheless, among the faculty in all these places I find a similar spirit of inquiry, devotion, and heartfelt desire to be good disciples of Jesus Christ and a deep commitment to teach others on the pathways of discipleship.

In the southern hemisphere, theological students are usually young, as compared to students in the North. The potential is awesome! Dedicated, gifted (and often unrecognized) educators have the privilege and responsibility of taking the unformed clay of young students and molding it into effective Christian men and women. The joy and reward for the teacher is to see some of these young people become leaders in Christian work in their own countries and beyond.

For many years I have heard well meaning persons suggest that if only we in the North and the West could hear a theological perspective from Asia, Latin America or Africa, we would have new and powerful insights that would enable us to better understand the Scriptures, our faith, and our Christian witness. Despairing of "tired" theology from the North and the West, they have declared that previously suppressed voices would produce emphases which could enlighten the whole Church.

It is true that from time to time, an historical, socioeconomic or political context will bring about a situation that will produce profound theological understanding that will shake the church and cause it to re-examine many of its theological presuppositions. Such teaching has emerged in the past out of Asia, and out of Latin America. But that was not the purpose of a special set of meetings in Buenos Aires, Argentina, during August 1995 as part of the Baptist World Congress meetings.

Baptist theologians gathered in Buenos Aires to talk about the contextualizing of the gospel in the various cultures of the southern hemisphere. Those who prepared papers wanted to share how the study of theology is pursued in their own contexts, cultures, and languages.

Perceptive readers will benefit from the different nuances, the fresh approaches, and the clear exposition in the papers from the different continents. We will all be forced to recognize that the eternal message of the gospel must be proclaimed and demonstrated in ways that make sense to the people of every nation, and in ways that are meaningful to them.

The papers that make up this book will be a valuable contribution to Baptists's (and others) awareness of what is happening in theological education throughout the world. These papers represent the contributions from a small number of theological educators from the southern hemisphere who were invited to submit papers to the seminar. The seminar took place at *Seminario Internacional Teológico Bautista,* the theological seminary of the Evangelical Baptist Convention of Argentina. Theological educators from all over the world attended the conference.

The seminar was a regional follow-up to the Baptist World Alliance's international conference on theological education, which was held in Johannesburg, South Africa in July, 1993. Every five years the Baptist World Alliance calls its theological educators together for an international conference in some part of the world. These BICTE conferences have been held successively in Ridgecrest, North Carolina, USA (1982) at Los Angeles, California, USA (1985), Zagreb, Yugoslavia (1989) and then in Johannesburg. The next one is scheduled for Vancouver in July, 1997.

In Johannesburg it was noted that many able theological educators from the southern hemisphere were unable to attend and, therefore, the wider Baptist family was denied their insights and responses. Consequently, it was decided to focus on theological voices from the South during the Baptist World Congress meetings in Buenos Aires in August 1995. The enthusiasm of those who participated, and the finished product, suggest that this was a good way to provide a forum that enabled Baptist voices from the South to be heard.

The Baptist World Alliance appreciates all who prepared papers, the leaders of the BWA's Academic and Theological Education workgroup who conducted the seminar, and Mercer University Press for publishing the papers. We hope that Christians every where can benefit from "hearing" the contemporary gospel accents found in these papers.

Introduction

Contextual Theology and Global Baptists

Richard F. Wilson

Since the early 1970s the idea of contextual theology has been closely associated with those expressions of political theology commonly called Liberation Theology, or theologies of liberation.[1] The close association is unfortunate. At its heart all theology is contextual. Any and every attempt to speak meaningfully about God in relation to the created order and human history includes a distinct point of view, a context that shapes confession. Defending the claim that all theology is contextual is not a difficult task. Even a casual look at scripture and Christian traditions requires acknowledging the shaping influences of the particular contexts out of which confessions of faith emerged.

ALL THEOLOGY IS CONTEXTUAL

Contexts in Scripture

The Old Testament, for example, includes two very different versions of the rise and fall of the monarchy in ancient Israel. The more elaborate version, usually referred to as the Deuteronomic History, found in the books of Joshua, Judges, Samuel and Kings, puts primary emphasis upon the establishment of the Davidic Covenant. Taking the notions of reward and punishment clearly articulated in the deuteronomic scroll discovered during the days of the reign of Josiah (see 2 Kings 22–23), the historians of the monarchy explored both the distant and immediate contexts out of which the Davidic dynasty came to be. The dramas of the Exodus event and the subsequent settlement of Canaan provided the broadest frame for the story. The failures of the judges and Saul—the experimental first king of Israel— provided a more narrow frame for the story of how David became King and, more importantly, how the covenant associated with David provided a sure foundation for the monarchy. Even when the monarchy crumbled, the foundation for the monarchy remained, transformed into a dynamic messianism that carried the descendants of Abraham and Sarah through the Exile and beyond.

At issue is the context from which the Deuteronomic History was shaped. Conceived and born during the height of Josiah's Reform, and gathering up the memory of the archetypical King David, this history sharply interprets divine presence in and through the King. David is the model for Josiah: "He did what was right in the sight of the LORD, and walked in all the way of his father David; he did not turn aside to the right or to the left" (2 Kings 22.2); in the end, however, Josiah surpassed David: "Before him there was no king like him, who turned to the LORD with all his heart, with all his soul, and with all his might, according to all the law of Moses; nor did any like him arise after him" (2 Kings 23.25).

The Deuteronomic Historian places emphasis on the person of the king. David is the promise and Josiah is the fulfillment; between them the monarchy flourishes and becomes the best way to confess that God is at work in the world.

There is another history in the Old Testament, however. Often referred to either as the Priestly History, or the work of the Chronicler, spanning 1 Chronicles through Nehemiah,[2] this second version of the rise and fall of the monarchy is framed by a different set of circumstances. It begins with a sweeping review of the lineage of the sons of Jacob (1 Chron 2–8), with special attention given to the priestly tribe of Levi (1 Chron 6) and an insertion of the line of David (1 Chron 3). The story of the monarchy from David primarily is told in light of the worship life of Israel and Judah, with particular emphasis upon the Temple.

The story of the end of the monarchy puts emphasis upon the failure of the kings of Judah to appreciate the presence of God in the Temple. The monarchy failed, to be sure, but the Temple remained the place where God could be seen and known. That the main emphasis in the Priestly History falls on the Temple is seen in the conclusion of 2 Chronicles (which also is the conclusion of the Hebrew Bible) where the Edict of Cyrus makes way for the Temple to be rebuilt in Jerusalem. The edict also plays a prominent role in the opening chapter of Ezra.

The Chronicler clearly reflects upon the presence of God in history from the point of view of the Exile. That context shapes the nature of the theology found in the books of Chronicles, Ezra, and

Nehemiah. The emphasis of the Chronicler does not fall on the King, because the monarchy is gone. The emphasis does fall on the place the kings had seen and known the presence of God: the Temple.

Taken together the Deuteronomic and Priestly Histories from the Old Testament provide examples of how scripture itself develops contextual theologies. Seen and understood side-by-side, the Deuteronomic and Priestly Histories also demonstrate the importance and value of cooperative narrative contexts. The emphasis on the person of the king in the Deuteronomist finds a corrective balance in the emphasis on the place of God's presence in the Chronicler. That different settings in history provide different emphases in confessing the presence of God is apparent. Furthermore, there is a strong indication that authentic theology requires at least a pair of contexts in order to provide balance to confessions of how and where God may be known.

In the New Testament the contextual shaping of theological confessions is most clearly seen in a comparison of the four Gospels. The first three Gospels—Matthew, Mark, and Luke—share a common point of view as they tell the Jesus story. Because of the common perspective the first three Gospels are called "synoptic" (from a pair of Greek terms: *syn*, meeting "with" and *optic*, meaning "eye"); they look at the story of Jesus with the same eye.

What Matthew, Mark, and Luke see is the way Jesus of Nazareth teaches and relates to people. More than anything else in the synoptic Gospels Jesus is one who preaches the kingdom of God in a way that is reminiscent of the great prophets of Israel's past, and the compelling prophet of his day, John the Baptizer (see Mark 1.14-15). Jesus in the synoptic Gospels is known by what he does: he explicitly proclaims the kingdom, he embodies the kingdom's presence through wonders of healing and exorcisms, and he illustrates the truths of the kingdom through proverbs and parables.

Taken as a whole the synoptic Gospels offer a glimpse of the contexts from which and for which they were written. The synoptic Gospel writers confessed the presence of God through Jesus of Nazareth's words and deeds. On the basis of those portrayals of word and deed the communities from which and for which the synoptic Gospels were written could conclude, with Peter and the Roman centurion, that Jesus of Nazareth is the Christ, the Son of the living God (see Matt 16.16 and parallels, and Mark 15.39).

Taken separately the synoptic Gospels also reveal particular aspects of the contexts from which and for which they were written. For example, comparing the beatitudes "Blessed are the poor in spirit, for theirs in the kingdom of God" and "Blessed are those who mourn, for they will be comforted" from Matthew's Gospel (5.3-4) to the be- atitudes in the Gospel of Luke, "Blessed are you who are poor, for yours is the kingdom of God" and "Blessed are you who are hungry now, for you will be filled" (Luke 6.20-21) demonstrates that there was a different economic context for each Gospel. Echoing what was claimed above in light of the balance struck between the contextual theologies of the Deuteronomist and the Chronicler in the Old Tes- tament, a theology of the kingdom of God needs both a figurative and a literal emphasis. The Gospels of Matthew and Luke offer such a bal- ance within the context of a synoptic portrayal of Jesus as "the Christ, the Son of the living God."

In the same way that the Old Testament does not offer a single perspective on the rise and fall of the Davidic monarchy, neither does the New Testament present a monotone story of Jesus. The picture of Jesus in the synoptic Gospels as one who does is balanced by the Gospel of John's depiction of Jesus as one who is. Throughout the Fourth Gospel Jesus, and others, makes claims of identity. Seven times Jesus utters an "I am" saying (e.g., "I am the bread of life" [John 6.35], and "I am the resurrection and the life" [John 11.25]). Of Jesus others make confessions such as "[Y]ou are the Son of God! You are the King of Israel!" (John 1.49), and "[Y]ou are the Holy One of God" (John 6.69). The overwhelming emphasis in the Fourth Gospel is one who Jesus is rather than what Jesus does.

Who Jesus is and what Jesus does are both important. Emphasiz- ing one over the other tells the contemporary reader as much about the story-tellers as it does the story of Jesus. The story as told also discloses something of the context in which the story took shape. Having both approaches to the Jesus story serves to balance the im- portance of the who and what about Jesus. Again we have seen that authentic theology requires at least a pair of contexts in order to pro- vide balance to confessions of how and where God may be known.

Contexts in Tradition

From the second century through the twentieth century Christian theology has been articulated through particular traditions. Out of well-defined contexts theological confessions were shaped in ways that gave rise to traditions. The earliest traditions emerged out of lin- guistic and philosophical settings. So we speak of the Greek and Latin

Fathers, tacitly noting that the language in which theology is pursued has a significant influence upon both what is confessed and how the confession is made. We refer to the Gnostic theologians or the Neo-platonists, again underscoring that a philosophical bent also bends confession.

By the height of the medieval period ways of thinking and acting theologically were almost exclusively sequestered by an adjective that paid homage to a well-defined tradition, many of which were credited to a well know theologian. Thus there were Augustinian theologians, Benedictine monks, Franciscan friars, and so on. Each adjective served to restrict and focus the larger tasks of theology throughout the church.

The medieval synthesis of theology, philosophy, and orders was temporarily broken by the rise of the Reformation, but within a generation a whole new set of theological adjectives exposed the traditional bearings of the Protestants (and the Roman Catholics who were already hard at work repairing the perceived damages wrought by the reformers). Luther was taken on by the Lutherans, Calvin was the darling of the Calvinists, and Arminius was hailed by the Arminians; and each group seemed oblivious to the fact that their contexts of protest had shaped its very identity within the larger church.

The contextualizing of theology along the lines of traditions, whether they emanate from powerful influences of thought or action, continues into the contemporary era. It is not enough these days, so it seems, to claim to be a Christian theologian of word and deed. Inevitably the theologian is asked, "And what kind of theologian are you?" The clearest of replies requires identifying with particular traditions that have been scrutinized by various segments of the church. The adjectives that limit theology have become as important (if not more important) than the theological confessions themselves. Philosophical positions still find their way into adjectives: Process theology, Existential theology, Thomistic theology. Sectarian positions also shape the types of confessions pursued: Methodist theology, Pentecostal theology, Baptist theology. Even hermeneutical methods take on the power of the adjective: narrative theology, evangelical theology, theology of the oppressed.

The foregoing panorama of theological traditions is representative rather than comprehensive. The point is to see that all theology is shaped by the very traditions that refine and preserve it. Keeping sight of the fact that traditions shape theology as powerfully as theology shapes traditions is, in a word, a reminder that all theol-

ogy is contextual. Because that is so, theologians at least have a responsibility to be aware of the tradition—or traditions—that shapes
them. To pursue theology any other way is to pursue theology na-
ively and inadequately.

Contexts in Culture

While scripture and traditions are the more obvious places where
contexts shape theology, culture is the most pervasive shaping influence. Culture is the place where all perspectives meet and vie for a
chance to set the standards of value, character, thought, and practice.
Because culture is the most pervasive shaping influence of theology it
is often the least recognized and discussed, akin to the common saying
"I cannot see the forest for the trees." Culture as a shaping influence
becomes visible, most often, when cultures come into conflict over
what was assumed to be a universal truth.

Since the middle of the twentieth century, at least, theologians
have pondered the various ways Christian confession encounters prevailing culture. H. Richard Niebhur's classic study *Christ and Culture*[3]
remains a benchmark for all who want to join the discussion. The five
ways of interpreting the intersections of Christ and culture Niebuhr
developed were primarily attempts to explore the political implications the gospel took on through western tradition. In the process,
however, Niebuhr opened the door to continuing discussions about
how the gospel and culture in its breadth and depth react to one another. In the contemporary conversations the focus of attention has
shifted to culture as context. To that subject we now turn.

TYPES OF CONTEXTUAL THEOLOGY

Stephen B. Bevans, theologian, missionary, and teacher, provides
valuable assistance for those who would struggle with the reality of
contextual theology at the end of the twentieth century. In *Models of
Contextual Theology*[4] Bevans describes five models for understanding
contextual theology, cautioning his readers to recognized that models
"are not mirrors of a reality" that can be hung on the wall for the
purpose of study, but are "ideal types...or abstractions formed from
concrete positions."[5] Models are tools that aid in the understanding of

truth, but the truth they illuminate is finally larger than any model used to approach it.

The remainder of this section relies upon the good work of Bevans and his description of contemporary models of contextual theology. The five types of models include a "translation model," an "anthropological model," a "praxis model," a "synthetic model," and a "transcendental model."[6]

A Translation Model

"Translation" suggests the movement from one language system to another, with the primary intent of maintaining the meaning of the words that are used. A translation model of contextual theology rests on the twin assumptions that the gospel may be reduced to a core of meaning, and that all cultures share a similar structure of meaning and communication. The core of meaning emphasized by those who employ a translation model for theology is heavily quantitative and propositional. What is at stake is the introduction of the facts and concepts of the gospel to a context where the gospel was previously unknown.

Missionary activity—at least at its historical point of origin—tends toward a translation model. Thus the "context" to be understood is the target culture and not the delivery culture. A translation model moves from an accepted core of meaning found in scripture and traditions toward a culture perceived to be "in need" of the gospel in a particular form.

An Anthropological Model

If a translation model described above is primarily interested in preserving a core of meaning found in scripture and traditions, then an anthropological model strives for the preservation of the uniqueness of any culture where the gospel takes root and grows toward maturity. Since God is the creator of the world, and humanity, there must be something of God in every culture (echoes of Rom 1–2 and Jn 1.1–18). An anthropological model of contextual theology begins with an affirmation of potential goodness of humanity and the culture(s) they establish.

A theologian who employs an anthropological model recognizes that the foundational work of proclaiming the gospel is learning so much about a culture that she or he can become as full a participant as possible in the culture. Related to the foundational work of learning the culture is the explicit theological task of discerning the presence of God within the culture.

A Praxis Model

Between the models of contextual theology described above as "translation" and "anthropological" falls a praxis model; this model leans toward an anthropological model, however. The term "praxis" is generally associated with the theologies of liberation that emerged in the late 1960s and early 1970s[7] and, through over use, has been deprived of its force. "Praxis" is not merely a sophisticated synonym for "practice" or "action." The force of the term, and the focus of this model, is the interplay among thinking and living, and doing and being. "Praxis is a technical term...which denotes a method or model for thinking in general, and a method or model of theology in particular."[8]

Employing a praxis model of contextual theology includes expecting and accepting that authentic theological pursuits are constantly moving between informed and committed responses to human need and reflections upon how the responses clarify and reshape confessions of faith. Culture, then, is the context within which the praxis model operates. Unlike translation and anthropological models, however, culture is neither a target to be hit (as with a translation model) nor a goal to be achieved (as with an anthropological model). In a praxis model culture is a dynamic reality that is going to change with or without theological influence and, therefore, becoming involved with culture is a theological mandate.

A Synthetic Model

A synthetic model of contextual theology also falls between models of translation and anthropological shape, but is more centrist than a praxis model. The theologian working with a synthetic model is first of all interested in dialogue between and among the features of the gospel and culture. As much as is possible a synthetic model affirms the uniqueness of the gospel rooted in scripture and traditions, and the uniqueness of culture as a composite of centuries of growth and change. Holding the uniqueness of both the gospel and culture in tension, this model strives for the theological maturity that can emerge out of honest conversation about the ways the gospel and culture mutually pursue freedom and wholeness.

Those who are most clearly identified with a synthetic model are not synthesizers in the sense of creating something artificial. Instead they are classical synthesizers who can appeal to the values of two very different realities—such as the gospel and culture—with the goal of incorporating the best of each reality in a third. Depending upon the particulars of a situation a synthesizer may emphasize a distinct point of the gospel, while in a another situation she or he may emphasize a distinct point of culture. The goal is not to rank the contributions of the gospel and culture, but rather to incorporate the values of the gospel and culture when they are most appropriate.

A Transcendental Model

Bevans's last model is a transcendental model, drawing from the broad philosophical and theological ideas that began with Immanuel Kant. At the beginning of the nineteenth century Kant shattered the notions of a reality that could be known objectively. For Kant and his followers, both in philosophy and theology, a knowing subject is the only context in which to encounter that which is true and enduring. A transcendental model places a significant emphasis upon personal experience and the conviction that God can, and does, disclose God's presence and character to individuals.

While a transcendental model appears to be the most spiritually oriented of the five Bevans articulates because of its sharp concentration upon the individual as a believing subject, it is a spirituality that is not necessarily accountable to scripture and traditions. This model is so removed from any theological content that it is hard to say how a transcendental model differs from theological relativism.[9]

Contextual Theology and Global Baptists

The models described above provide points of departure to explore the new horizon of Baptist theologies in context. The horizon stretches before us and behind us because until now there have been no attempts to explore Baptist confession and practice in light of contextual theology. Historically Baptists have hailed from Europe, and then the United States. When Baptists began to move into other areas of the world it was as missionaries, either formally appointed or on their own.

Without doubt the earliest Baptist missionaries in Africa, Asia, Southeast Asia, and Latin America would have fit well into a "translation model" as described above. Well into the twentieth century the task of Baptists presenting the gospel was little more than bringing the gospel to places it had not been before, with on thought given to the possibility that the gospel was wrapped in the cultural garbs of Europe and North America.

As missions became established and missionaries began to feel more "at home" in new cultures, some missionaries began wondering whether the gospel they proclaimed was as translatable as they once believed. The beginnings of an "anthropological model" for theology could be seen when Baptist missionaries from Europe and North America began adopting the customs of their new-found homes. In doing so they became aware of the value of the cultures they had come to evangelize and, in turn, became less interested in converting the culture of Africa or Latin America into a mirror of the culture in the North American South.

What is to be found on the horizon before us is an adventure waiting. One thing is certain: the developments in Baptist contextual theology spawned in 1993 at a Johannesburg, South Africa conference for Baptist theologians and educators, and the first-ever conference where Baptists from south of the equator were encouraged to articulate the meaning of the gospel from a cultural perspective, held in Buenos Aires, Argentina in 1995 have brought the horizon closer. The adventure waiting will not wait much longer.

The essays that follow may be the first chapter to be written on the subject of contextual theology and global Baptists. Enough about what may be. Forge ahead and find out what is.

Notes

[1]The terms "Liberation Theology" and "theologies of liberation" are not synonymous. The singular term with capital letters gives the impression that a "school" of theology was born and continues to exist, a school that shares well defined methods, perspectives, and goals. The plural term with lower case letters indicates the emergence of diverse theological expressions from equally diverse perspectives. While the theologies of liberation that came to prominence in the late 1960s and the early 1970s shared the conviction that a truly biblical theology demands working for social justice, the theologies of liberation did not emerge as synthetic responses to the formal expressions of theology that preceded them, nor did they spring from established academic centers. Despite the popularity of the term Liberation Theology, the second term, theologies of liberation, more accurately describes the history and continuing growth of political and social theologies that see justice as a primary concern of the gospel.

[2]Until recently the unity of 1 Chronicles–Nehemiah was widely held. Despite contemporary questions about authorship and style there is wide agreement that the themes of the four books (which are but two books in the Hebrew Bible) form a composite perspective of the misfortunes and hopes of Judah seen from the point of view of the Edict of Cyrus that brought an end to the Exile. See David A. Smith, "Ezra–Nehemiah," *Mercer Commentary on the Bible*, Watson E. Mills and Richard F. Wilson, eds. (Macon, Georgia: Mercer University Press, 1995), 373.

[3]H. Richard Niebuhr, *Christ and Culture* (New York: Charles Scribner's Sons, 1951).

[4]Stephen B. Bevans, *Models of Contextual Theology* (Maryknoll, New York: Orbis Books, 1992).

[5]Ibid., 24.

[6]This section will only begin to describe the models Bevans constructs from years of experience and reflection. Interested readers should consult Bevans for clarification and elaboration. I have intentionally avoided using Bevans's language, except when it is unavoidable, for fear of repeating less than I should. The intent of presenting the models is descriptive.

[7]See note 1 above.

[8]Ibid., 64.

[9]Ibid., 102.

Let Us Speak Our-selves

Daniel Carro

My vision for this conference on contextual theology from the South is to present to the theological world, particularly to our "northern" theological friends, a view of theological labors as seen from the perspective of the peoples who live and toil below the equatorial line of privileges.

That the world looks different when seen from the South is indisputable. "Southern" theologians, therefore, have a responsibility to confess the meaning and tasks of theology to our colleagues who live above the equator.

Our conference, first of all, is a commitment and a call to theologians living in the South: "Let us speak our–selves!" But we do not wish only to speak among our–selves. We want to share our confessions and commitments with our northern friends and colleagues.

LET US

In general, North Atlantic theologies are regarded as "central theologies," while other expressions (e.g., liberation theologies, black theologies, feminist theologies) are discerned as peripheral to the main issues of theology. When theologies from the periphery have gained notice, they have been popularized for the world by theologians of the "center." The repackaging of southern theologies includes both subtraction and addition of certain elements to make them more understandable and affective to "central theologies."[1] In such instances, "southern" theologies have suffered in silence through years of misinterpretations and distorted characterizations.

Our assignment in this conference is to demonstrate clearly why the concept of "central" and "peripheral" theologies is biased and prejudicial. If the meaning and tasks of theology are to be holistic, then all confessions should be heard and explored. An additional challenge of our conference will be to show how all theologies, even the "central" ones, are unavoidably contextual.

Perhaps some of our "northern" brothers and sisters, upon reading the title of this introduction, thought we were asking their permission to theologize. Let us make it clear from the very beginning: We are not asking for permission to speak. Rather we offer a fraternal appeal to let us speak from our–selves and for our–selves.

Neither should this conference be seen as an attempt to engage in a contentious theology, or in another theological monologue. On the contrary, we invite our "northern" brothers and sisters to participate in a dialogue. We have been listening to and following their monologue for a long time. Now we will speak. Our hope is that they will listen. Our brothers and sisters will have an opportunity to answer, if they desire. When they do, we will listen. In the listening and speaking together, we will have dialogue.

A third aspect of our conference is a protest against unwanted and unnecessary interference in the development of our "southern" theologies. It should be a declaration of theological independence, a cry of determination, an assertion of willful resolution. Please, let us "do our theology" within the integrity of our contexts.

Perhaps some of our "northern" friends think our theologies do not sound "mature." Perhaps they think that if we are left alone we will spoil the theological enterprise. But if they do not listen as we think for our-selves, and if they continue misinterpreting the nature of our confessions of faith, and continually rephrase our contextual theologies in categories that fit the theologies of the North Atlantic, then the development of contextual theologies that address our "southern" circumstances will be at least deferred. If that happens, the whole world will lack our theological perspectives and, therefore, the meaning and talks of theology will be less than it should.

Our point of view may appear as unimportant to our brothers and sisters in the North, but it is very important to us. What may appear peripheral to those pursuing theology in the North is indeed central to those of us pursuing the gospel in Africa, Asia, Southeast Asia, and Latin America. We all live in a whole world. Let us strive to hear a whole gospel.

LET *US*

Suppose for a moment that those who shape "central" theologies give us some space. Let us dream that "southerners" are no longer patronized or discriminated against. Are we ready to speak out for our–selves? Are we ready to let our thinking flow along its natured courses without looking for approval from our northern friends? Are we ready to pursue the meaning and tasks of theology "from scratch"? Are we ready to abandon Egypt with its onions and garlic, and experience the isolation, danger and solitude of the desert?

Our conference needs to be a time and place where we incite our desire to speak for our–selves. We "southerners" hide too often behind a protective curtain of noninvolvement. We criticize the theologies of others, but we have not struggled to give birth to our own. If Jesus is to be seen through us, we must allow the incarnational word to speak from the abyss of our own existence. Let us do it. Let us do it now. Our conference is an invitation and an opportunity to begin.

LET US *SPEAK*

A beloved Argentine pastor, who was president of our Argentine Baptist Convention many times, used to say to long lines of people wanting to speak: "There are two kinds of speakers. Those who have something to say, and there are those who have to say something. We want to hear the first." Our conference is for those who have something to say. We invite them to share their thoughts, their concerns, their hopes, their strengths and weaknesses, and their understanding of the gospel. We invite them to share their perception of God, their *theology*.

LET US SPEAK *OUR–SELVES*

My initial phrasing of the invitation to participate in this conference was: "Let us speak our minds." Now I know that we need to do more than speak our minds. Our hearts "have many reasons that reason knows not of." Our wills have many desires unfulfilled. Our strengths have many challenges that have not been confronted. Our souls have many longings that remain unsatisfied. So, let us articulate our–selves, let us vocalize our whole beings, and let us pronounce our complete humanity in the face of our understanding of the gospel.

Gospel, God-spell, Theo-logy, is the place of encounter of two beings: God and us. God (*theo*) is disclosed in our logos (*logy*). God gave us the *logos*, the word; and God is the eternal Logos, the Word. Jesus Christ, as the incarnate logos of God, has done for us the ultimate exegesis of the nature of God. To speak about God in light of the gospel is nothing else than to speak about our–selves and the way we have come to understand in finite words such an infinite Word.

Let us speak of God and the gospel with our whole beings. Let our minds catch as clearly as possible God's demands. Let our hearts rejoice in the hope of God's new day to come. Let our wills dream of meeting God's challenge. Let our souls be filled only with God, and by God's word. Let our faith be illumined and discerned through our theology. Let us do it in full accord with our own contexts.

To our "northern" friends and the world-at-large we say: Listen! Listen to what the gospel means to us in Africa, in Asia, in Southeast Asia, and in Latin America.

To our "southern" friends we say: Let us speak for ourselves what the gospel means to us. Let us pronounce a *theology* that makes sense, one that is truly meaningful to us.

NOTES

[1]See, for example, Raymond McAfee Brown, *Theology in a New Key* (Philadelphia: Westminster Press, 1978) and Harvey Cox, *The Silencing of Leonardo Boff* (Oak Park, Illinois: Meyer Stone Books, 1988).

Part One
Accents from Africa

A Gospel of Community, Compassion, and Continuity

Douglas Waruta

This paper is an attempt to highlight the theological and other struggles that Africans are going through. Africa remains on the periphery of economic, political, social, technological, and even theological/religious/ecclesial matters. Our continent is on the fringes of the so-called modern world to the extent that we not only identify with the Third World, but we may rightly be called the Third World of the Third World. From the edge of the edge, this paper calls for a theology for the outsiders, for the recipients of whatever others in our world choose to offer as, and for those to be found by the "highways and hedges" outside the city (Luke 14.23). It is our conviction as African Christians, at least a significant number of us, that an Afrocentric understanding of the gospel of Jesus Christ is necessary, if our people are going to live in hope. The following pages highlight some of these concerns that press on Africans, so that those who wish to ask us what we believe may begin to understand our struggles toward Christian solidarity and common Christian purpose.

An Afrocentric Understanding of the Gospel

Last December I was invited to address the Annual Assembly of the Baptist Convention of Southern Africa. I was excited not only because I was going to address, and have fellowship with my brothers and sisters during their first Assembly as a free people in a free and democratic South Africa, I was also excited by their vision, a vision which no other African Christian group I have known has ever expressed so clearly as our South African Baptists have done. Their mission statement is original and authentic:

> The Baptist convention of South Africa is a fellowship of member churches *whose mission is to develop and proclaim a holistic, Afrocentric, and participatory understanding of the Gospel of Jesus Christ* and thereby equip its constituencies to facilitate the dynamic transformation of societies (emphasis added).

There is only one gospel of Jesus Christ, the one gospel that invites all humanity to the banquet of the kingdom, the one gospel that calls mankind and the whole of creation to be reconciled to God and to each other. Yet the one gospel is understood differently by the people of God throughout its history. People have emphasized different aspects of the one gospel as their contexts have demanded, and as they have experienced the impact of the gospel in daily living.

The history of the church is characterized by different understandings, and even distortions of the gospel of Jesus Christ. One of the biggest distortions of the gospel is its historical Western Magisterial Captivity that occurred when the Christian faith became a religion of power and authority, domination and conquest of other peoples in the name of Christ. The sixteenth century Protestant Reformation, with all of its very noble intentions of reclaiming the gospel from the Magisterial Captivity of Rome, finally could not pull the gospel out of the pervasive influence of Western Christendom. Until now we of the periphery have come to expect from the historical background a gospel of power and authority to continue. Our experience has been with a Christianity of physical, psychological and spiritual conquest of others, instead of a gospel of liberation and love. It is this background that necessitates a rereading of the gospel story from the perspective of those on the sidelines. What is demanded is a new hermeneutics of positive suspicion of the historical understanding of the use of the gospel in order to facilitate a genuine, authentic and liberating understanding of the gospel in contemporary Africa.

An Afrocentric understanding of the gospel does not deny European, Asiatic, American, or Caribbean Christians—or any others—the privilege to articulate what it means to be a Christian in their own contexts. Indeed, when all of us engage in the quest for a genuine understanding of the gospel of Christ, then and only then can we truly have a global perspective of the gospel which will not only help us to appreciate and experience the wealth of the one gospel, but also appreciate each other and enter into true fellowship with each other. As it is now, the western hegemonic understanding of the gospel, and the tendency to dictate its understanding and emphases to the rest of the world, is untenable and unacceptable. Christian faith must be freed from such conditions.

In my view, this is what impressed our brothers and sisters in South Africa. After experiencing centuries of a dominating and oppressive western Christendom, they arrived at a mission statement that spells out their commitment to an Afrocentric understanding of the gospel. I am grateful to them for provoking me to engage in this quest afresh.

In Africa there is a new movement that is searching for a more authentic understanding and expression of our heritage. African peoples, perhaps more than other peoples, have been other-defined people. We not only carry other people's names, ideologies, and theologies, but our continent was named by outsiders, and even our nations were carved out named and shaped by others. For too long we have been treated as a cultural, spiritual, and intellectual table rasa upon which everyone wants to put his mark. We are Anglicans, Lutherans, Baptists, Presbyterians, Catholics, Methodist, Adventists and, in recent years, Evangelicals, Ecumenicals, Fundamentalists, Pentecostals, Charismatics (and everything else under the sun) not because we have chosen to be so, but because some outside influence has given us the labels we carry. Worst of all, we are largely not even conscious of our inauthenticity! Sometimes when we become conscious of this fact, we find it more convenient to ignore the truth and to continue to trudge along in the borrowed and heavy garbs and armaments of the mighty Saul!

Afrocentric understanding of the gospel is an attempt to reread the gospel from a deliberate Africa–centered perspective, and in doing so, to break the hermeneutic hegemony and ideological strangle hold that historical western Christendom has long enjoyed. By engaging an Afrocentric understanding of the gospel we do not intend to rewrite the gospel, but to strip it of this western ideological, abstract, dominating mentality in order to enjoy the freedom and blessings the gospel is capable of providing to all who come to know the good news of

Christ. We want to go beyond the sphere of the relatively abstract, authoritarian, and often arrogant presentation of the gospel to a sphere characterized by humility, love, and hope for those who are still in the periphery. We want to read the rarely read story of the God of the Bible, the God of Jesus Christ who begins his story not from the centers of power, but from the position of the periphery. Reading the Bible, both the Old and the New Testaments, the reality of the God of peripheral peoples is clearer than we ever thought or dared to understand.

This story is best brought to us in the Gospel of Luke which is the classic text for the peripheral peoples. Mary declares the collapse of the mighty and the rising of those from the periphery. When Jesus is born, it is among periphery people, the shepherds who first hear the good news "which shall be for all peoples." Later Jesus announces the inauguration of his ministry in the words of Isaiah 61, that the good news is for the peripheral peoples, the wretched of the earth. Jesus re-members, reconnects and reunites the mission of God of the oppressed. The rest of the gospel is a catalogue of the hope for those on the outside, the good Samaritan, Lazarus, the prodigal son, Zaccheus, the afflicted and the disinherited. And finally, Jesus is crucified not only outside the city, but also between peripheral nonentities, one of whom who became the first to enter paradise. How this very clear gospel of the periphery has come to be so lost, so hidden, so different and so removed from those for whom it was intended is one of the marvels of historical Christianity. For most contemporary Christians influenced by historical western Christianity—from con-servatives to the liberals, from the Charismatics to the Fundam-entalists, from Evangelicals to the Ecumenicals, from the Prot-estants to the Catholics—the gospel of Christ has come to be identified, with power and not love, with judgement and not mercy, with domination and not service, with majesty and not humility, with pomp and extravagance rather than with a community of love and kindness. Christianity in its historical western setting is no longer attractive or meaningful to many who live elsewhere; one can easily see why it also has become largely irrelevant in the West. As Africans, unless we recover the true spirit of the gospel of Christ, the gospel of the God of the people in the periphery, this pompous worldly and glorious Christianity of might will soon be relegated to irrelevance even by those in the periphery to whom it was first addressed.

Life on the Periphery: the African Situation

The African situation is unique. Africa is a continent that demands innovative and bold decisions. Africa, a continent of 28 1/2 million square kilometers is the home of approximately one-half a billion people. Africa is considered to be the oldest continent and the place where archaeologists have found evidence that the first human beings existed before they were scattered to the other continents. Africa is the most pluralistic continent in our world, home of Caucasians, Asiatics, Semites, Hamites, and, of course, the predominant Negroid peoples. Over one thousand languages and dialects are spoken in Africa. At the same time, Africa is probably the most relaxed, uncomplicated, and psychologically sound continent where boisterous laughter is only punctuated by the anguish of poverty and oppression.

In material and human developments, Africa is considered extremely under developed. Two thirds of the poorest people on earth are Africans; eight of the ten poorest countries in the world are in Africa. Africa has an average of only $350 per capita income, compared with $21,530 in the developed industrial countries of the West (according to 1991 statistics). Africans are still dying of diseases that were eliminated in developed countries long ago. As an example, even though the center of attention in our world has shifted to the threat of the dreaded disease AIDS, malaria alone still claims over one million African lives a year.

Through slavery, colonialism and now neocolonialism, Africans have not been only the most exploited and oppressed peoples of the earth, the tragic reality is that they also have been the most dehumanized and humiliated. The dark color of the African people has come to be identified with not only poverty and misery, but as an explanation and excuse for regarding and treating the African people as inferior, subhuman creatures. Their capacity to develop into full-fledged human beings has not only been questioned, but also has been given a pseudo-scientific explanation by quite a few scholars from the dominant races. Worse still, many Africans have come to believe they are indeed inferior, especially when they compare themselves with the so-called developed nations. When Africans see their own lack of technological advancement, their poor management of time, resources and politics, their economic dependence on others, they too come to accept that perhaps it is true that they are inferior to the other races. The fact of the matter, however, is that the African condition has no racial basis, but is basically historical and environmental.

In spite of the grim picture of the current state of affairs, Africa's potential remains strong. Africa is endowed with great natural and human resources which have yet to be harnessed. Africa is a rich continent endowed with plenty of land, strategic mineral resources, great rivers, lakes and mountains, which are nearly inexhaustible sources of fresh water for irrigation. With its tropical climate, Africa could become the center of life-supporting activities for the rest of the world.

Today Africa is poor not because it lacks resources, but because its resources remain either largely untapped, or are tapped by and for the benefit of the peoples of other continents. The new way of exploiting the African resources is not necessarily through direct colonial domination, but through the prevailing world economic order in which multinational corporations, backed by powerful capitalist nations, dominate the global economy.

The African governments and organizations that should demand economic justice from the international community cannot do so, because most of them are run by despots whose interest is in personal power rather than the well being of the African people. Most of these despots, who came to power as a result of colonial systems and were supported generously by western powers at the heyday of the Cold War, are now being phased out, but Africa remains trapped in a political, cultural, and economic world dominated by forces outside the boundaries of the continent.

Even in religious terms, Africa remains a consumer of theological and ideological movements whose capacity to give hope to the African people are doubtful at best. There is a new scramble for Africa among all manner of dubious religious groups. Many of these groups call themselves Christian, but also groups associated with Islam, oriental religions and other stranger cults are attracting millions of African people. Sadly, these new religious groups are contributing to a new form of slavery, more devastating than the literal enslavement of Africans in the past. Yet Africans are embracing them with zeal, especially when they have the promise of financial advancement. Also, a new wave of Non-Governmental Organizations NGOs are flocking to Africa; some of them claim to be Christian. Their involvement in relief and development work has saved many lives in Africa, but the tragedy of the matter is that in spite of their activities and increase, the African people are worse off today then they ever were. In fact, NGOs in the name of the poor have become booming business, creating lucrative jobs for thousands of relief workers from the West. A book by Graham Hancock entitled *The Lords of Poverty*[1] presents shocking evidence of the scandal of helping the poor. No one underestimates the human calamity and misery experienced by people of the little country of Rwanda, for example, but one wonders what difference 157 NGOs make, each claiming to spend from thousands to millions of dollars for the benefit of the six million Rwandese people. One of the stories I heard recently in Uganda was that if you see a Pajero (luxury four wheel driven Japanese vehicle) likely it either belongs to a relief agency from a western government, or church agency, if it does not belong to one of a corrupt African politician. The fact that even Christian NGOs are not contributing much for the uplifting of African peoples is a frightening reality that our Christian friends around the world must come to term with. Worse still, many of these NGOs have such narrow agendas and questionable motives—and are foreign dominated—that they raise legitimate suspicions from genuinely concerned African people. How can we not remember the story of Lazarus and the Rich Man? And how can the rest of the world refuse to learn from the story?

African Responsibility

I do not wish to conclude an analysis of the plight of African people by placing only blame on outside forces. Most of African misery is self-inflicted. We have tolerated bad governments and even abetted their excesses by accepting them as legitimate. Our almost fatalistic and too accommodating tendency towards suffering and misery has been our greatest undoing. Our incapacity to plan well and to use the time to our advantage; and our frequent ineptitude in managing precious and scarce resources when we do take charge is our fault. Our poor stewardship of what God has given to us cannot be blamed on others, and we continue to pay dearly for it. As Africans, we have refused to grow up and become self-critical, and we have not cultivated a burning desire to change what must be changed in order to survive and prosper. Africans need to learn the lesson of the prodigal son!

We have refused to face reality, no matter how painful it may be, and we have hidden ourselves in the comfort of our dreams and wishes. We have lacked the moral courage to aim at greater heights of our existence, and we have tended to be satisfied with too little. Africans allow many good opportunities to slip through their fingers, seeming to think that there is an African time that can wait for them until they are ready to wake up. With all of the other peoples of the world, Africans must know that we live in a competitive world, and we must know that if we lose in the survival game, ultimately we have no one to blame but ourselves.

Africans even think we can hide in a narcotic type of religious fervor—for which many people especially in the western world are praising us for (because it did not work for them)—but in the long run will become an extremely costly hideout. We want to pray and change the world through prayer without work, that is, without paying the price of disciplined, industrious, and responsible living. We are embracing proponents of hideout religion without giving thought to it. We have refused on a wider scale to pursue excellence and innovative, creative living, and have satisfied ourselves with the efforts of others.

The point I am raising, and I should not have to belabor it too much, is that the greatest enemy of the African is the African. All other enemies succeed because of that basic fact; until we realize that we are the biggest problem to ourselves, we shall remain forever the "hewers of wood and drawers of water" (Josh 9) for other people. African culture also is blessed with positive qualities of community, compassion, cooperation, stamina, spirituality and celebration of life—characteristics we have refused to exploit and maximize for the well being of our children and continent. We must go back to our roots, to our essential selves, and critically take stock of who we really are. Then we must throw away the retrogressive qualities that

keep us down, and strive to recover the positive and noble characteristic from our rich heritage and unapologetically use them in the reconstruction of our distorted and defaced personality. By doing so, we
will be bringing out the very best of what is already there, that image
of God revealed to us through the scriptures and in Jesus Christ.

The Basis for an Afrocentric Interpretation of the Gospel

As we have observed, things are not well for Africans and their
continent. There is so much death and destruction that the world has
come to accept African calamities as normal and expected. The case
of Rwanda is the latest in the grim history of contemporary Africa.
African life has become extremely cheap and worthless in the eyes of
the majority of the people of the world, including Africans. As Christians we must refuse the current state of affairs. We must refuse to
accept death and destruction and lead our people into life. If biblical
faith and Christian faith has any validity, it must provide the African
people the way from death to life. An Afrocentric understanding of
the gospel must focus on life rather than death.

First, the biblical God, the God of Jesus Christ, we confess is the
Lord of the living. God is the author of life and not death. The gospel
story clearly shows what kind of God we have. When the children of
Israel were in Exile, their lives, faith and hope had been destroyed by
the might of Babylon. Some had given up the struggle. But this biblical
God promises them a hope and a future (Jer 29.11). In Jesus Christ,
God has come to us even in a more intimate way, giving us not merely
life, but "abundant life" (John 10.10). It is not the will of the creator
that God's children should live in misery and death. It is not God's will
that Africans remain an exploited, oppressed, and humiliated people.
African life (as well as all the other segments of humanity) is created
in the image of God. Those who have abused us have not abused only
us, but also they have abused our creator.

The heart of the good news is that God intends freedom, life,
prosperity and welfare for God's people. This central truth is the one
that led the African people to embrace Christianity. Africans did not
become Christians because it was brought by white missionaries and
white people. In fact many times Africans became Christians in spite

of the excesses of the white people. This is the miracle of the expansion of the gospel of God. It is the power of God unto salvation. Africans saw in this gospel the message of life, rather than the threat of death. When Africans read the Bible for themselves, they identified themselves with this God of life. Africans love life, where life is the theme, they will be there. They saw in Jesus Christ one who is pro-life. He heals sicknesses, casts out oppressive demons and makes people physically and spiritually strong. Africans came to love Jesus, and today Africa has a most lively church. Afrocentric interpretation of the gospel is first and foremost based on this God of life—the God who has a plan and promises a hope, and a future.

Secondly, an Afrocentric interpretation of the gospel proceeds from the nature of the African people. The black people of Africa are strong. The more you kill them, take them into slavery, impoverish them and do every manner of tricks to diminish them, they refuse to die, they refuse to be diminished. When millions were taken to the Americas and the Caribbean Islands as slaves, they continued to prosper. After three hundred years of servitude, Africans in the West have now become a force to reckon with. Our enemies have tried every trick to remove us so that they can take our continent for themselves, but they failed. They failed in the past, and will also fail in the future. Tell those who despise us that Africans may be bruised, and pulled down, but that they never stay down. Africans have and will come back.

Thirdly, Africans are among the most forgiving of all people. I am amazed at how Africans are able to embrace their former enemies and turn them into friends. In Kenya, our first President Jomo Kenyatta told unbelieving white settlers who had ruthlessly killed and exploited our people for decades that they will be forgiven. "We will forgive you," he said, "but we will not forget what you did to us." Many who had committed terrible atrocities on African people did not believe him, they ran south to Rhodesia (now Zimabawe) and to South Africa to continue their mayhem. But some of those who stayed in Kenya, as many did, thirty years later were elected as members of parliament.

An Afrocentric interpretation of the gospel should build on the forgiving spirit of the African people. Look at Ian Smith the man who destroyed thousands of Zimbabwe to maintain white privilege in

Zimbabwe. He is a free man walking in the streets of Harare without any harassment from the people he so ruthlessly treated. South Africa, could not have survived without a Mandela, an African in the true sense of the word, characterized by the spirit of forgiveness. After twenty-seven years in cruel prison, he embraced his former enemies and proclaimed forgiveness and reconciliation. Is not this the way of the gospel? Africans have such a wonderful spirit of forgiveness. That spirit should be included in the basis for an Afrocentric theology. This magnificent story of Africans is hardly told by many who see nothing good about Africa! We must tell this story—it is the story of a people of life and not death. We will forgive them, but we shall not forget. How can we forget even if we wanted to when we have all these marks of their oppression on our bodies and in our land?

Finally, the gospel of Jesus Christ calls us to proclaim freedom, peace and prosperity for the people. The biblical God in Jesus Christ promises shalom. The Hebrew word *shalom*, often translated "peace," means more than the absence of conflict and a life of justice and rest. The Jews and Arabs greet one another in this rich word of the *shalom*, often without realizing its original meaning and depth. The biblical God promises and gives the *shalom* to all people. When the risen Christ appeared to his disciples in the upper room, he wished them *shalom*. "My peace I leave with you."

Conclusion

> [Be not afraid (Africans)...]
> For behold I bring you good news of great joy
>   which will come to all people
> For to you is born this day in the city of David
>   A Savior who is Christ the Lord
> ...Glory to God in the Highest,
>   and on Earth peace (shalom) among men
>   with whom He is pleased (Luke 2.10-14).

I propose three goals African Christians must seek to achieve. These are community, compassion and continuity. An Afrocentric understanding of the gospel must incorporate these paradigms. The

African story is rooted in community life characterized by compassion (a feeling with) and continuity. Ours is a story which, in spite of external challenges and forces, has refused to go away. Its basic tenets are participation, protection and provision of the means of livelihood. Because, of these three characteristics, Africans have embraced the Christian faith because they identify with its promises to enhance the basic characteristics of life. They are often frustrated when, sometimes Christianity (particularly the Christianity of the center) fails to live up to these expectations. One of the reasons some African Christians start what is commonly known as Independent or African Instituted Churches is the frustration with the Christianity of the center. If Christianity is going to continue to have significant impact in Africa, it must be the basis upon which a new community of compassion and continuity is built. The Christian gospel interpreted from the periphery and away from the center is very powerful force at work in creation of the spiritual community Africa is looking for.

First, what do we mean by the community? We mean that the African community must be recreated and renewed. The Africa sense of community after colonialism and exploitation is distorted. Our rich cultural heritage had been described as primitive and pagan. Our children and our people have been subjected to an education, and even a religion, that make them feel bad and ashamed of themselves. A major psychological warfare has been waged against the very core of the African community, its self-esteem and dignity. In our struggle to start again, the place to begin is the restoration of the African pride and confidence in ourselves. African selfhood must be affirmed through a new educational system that affirms the African person all the way from the nursery school to the university. Churches should stop preaching as if the Africans are the worst of sinners. Africans are sinners, yes, but they are not the worst of sinners, as many have been made to believe. We must tell our children over and over again that they have the potential for the best of what is possible in humanity (of course they will hear of the worst). Our children must not hear of only the Idi Amins, the Bokasas, and other ruthless dictators we have had. They must be told the other, longer story of Albert Luthuli, the Mondlanes, the Nkrumas, the Kenyattas, the Mandelas, and the thousands of heroes who embody what is good in the African community.

The other, longer story can be found in every African community big and small.

The African sense of the community must be a broader and more inclusive one. The community, the new community must be based on those who share and cherish the values of life and hope and not on ethnicity, tribalism, and language groups. African community must expand and include people who share in the struggle for life, and who are brought together by their affirmations, convictions and the struggle for life. Africans should reject narrow-minded leaders who wish to reduce us to tribal groupings. That does not mean we cease to be Xhosas, Zulus, or Kikuyus, what it means is that as Xhosas, Zulus and Kikuyus we embrace each other and enhance each other because of our common humanity. We embrace not only those men and women from the African continent, but all humanity who join us in the cry and struggle to eliminate human misery and death in the world. Africans have always been an inclusive, hospitable people. The hospitable spirit should be a basis for building a new community, united for and in life. The church of Jesus Christ is the new community. We are brought together by the good news of great joy, which shall be for all people in whom God is pleased (Luke 2.10-14). From Africa a lesson should go into the world on what it means to be a community in a world where the sense of community has been destroyed by the culture of competitiveness and individualism.

In the new community every person will be given the opportunity to play his or her role. Members of the community who feel left out or disadvantaged should be given the opportunity to present their case. The new community must be an open, participatory, just and all-inclusive community. As a community comprised of the peripheral people, the struggling people, the new community will recognize and appreciate the plight of each member and each segment of the community, particularly those who have suffered most of the oppression.

Second, the African community will be characterized by compassion. The well-being of individuals and the entire community remain the *sunnum bonum* of the community. Compassion should go beyond sentiment and engage in the quest for the elimination of human misery, not in the short run, but permanently. Compassion should not be comprised of mere gestures of helping or alleviating poverty, but should build on strategies that go to the root of the causes of poverty in society, and seek to transform the causes of human misery. It is the compassion that does not only help the poor, but seeks to know why they are poor. The compassion we need in Africa should be different from the acts of charity that have become the style of our times, even among Christians.

The final recommendation for the prosperity of Africa is that of continuity. Africa must establish permanent institutions and structures which will improve the quality of life. The place to begin is with political systems that guarantee good and responsible governance. Without good government even the church of Jesus Christ cannot survive. In the past Africans have allowed the development of bad governments and have paid dearly for it. We must struggle for institutions that guarantee human and people's rights, accountability, and transparency. Justice in Africa must not only be done but be seen to be done.

On the African continent, we must endeavor to be competitive in a harsh world where the weak have no chance. It will be necessary for Africa to emphasize competence and hard work. Competence and hard work, with honesty, will take Africa far. In Africa we must reward competence and hard work handsomely in order to promote the same and ingrain in the mentality of our youth the values of merited success. For too long, Africa has stifled its talents, or allowed them to remain dormant, untapped, or undeveloped. With the abundance of human and natural resources, it is our management and effort capacity that is lacking to transform Africa from a bigger continent to one where life thrives in abundance.

As Africans, we must establish institutions of academic excellence for research in social and physical sciences, and put to use our best brains for the service of the African people and the world. Currently very little primary research is done in Africa. We have become mere consumers of other people's efforts at very high price. We should reject the notion that there is conflict or division between religion and sciences, religion and politics, religion and business, indeed, religion and life. African spirituality demands a unity of purpose in promoting life enhancing endeavors as they are all basically religious. In the mind of the African, there is no sacred and secular, for life is a unity and it is sacred.

May God bless Africa and all who love and defend her
May God bring His Shalom to all of us
Nkosi sikelel Africa
Mungu Ibariki Africa
God bless Africa
Amen.

NOTES

[1]Graham Hancock, *The Lords of Poverty: the power, prestige, and corruption of the international aid business* (New York: Atlantic Monthly Press, 1989).

A Gospel of *Edinyanga*

Harrison G. Olan'g

In 1962 a commentator observed: "Man outside Africa is confronted by an ever changing continent. Man inside Africa is caught up
in the change that is transforming the continent from day one to the
next."[1] Writing in 1995, an African theologian echoed the same idea:
"Contemporary Africa is undergoing rapid social transition with new
beliefs, norms and values introduced from outside, while the old traditions are having to be modified to suit changing circumstances."[2] The
church in Africa is a changing church in an ever changing society.

As the result of changes, Africa south of the Sahara is undergoing
myriad political, economic and social upheavals. Civil wars, inflation,
poverty, joblessness, drug smuggling, and ecological crisis are part of
everyday life. Furthermore, there appears to be corruption in all institutions, including Christian institutions. In the book of Romans we
can find a description which that is typical of contemporary Africa.

> They are all gone out of the way; they have together become unprofitable;
> there is none that does good, no, not one. Their throat is an open sepul-
> chre; with their tongues they have used deceit; the poison of asps is under
> their lips; whose mouth is full of cursing and bitterness. Their feet are swift
> to shed blood; destruction and misery are in their ways; and the ways of
> peace have they not known; there is no fear of God before their eyes (Rom
> 3.12-18 NKJV).

Writing on the mission of the church in Africa in the post–Cold
War era, Laurenti Magesa has pointed out that, "faced with this historical reality, it becomes essential to look at past, present and future
approaches of Christian evangelization from the perspective of the
sufferings and brutalization of Africa itself."[3] The categories of past,

present, and future are appropriate for establishing a context for understanding the gospel in Africa today.

The Past of Christian Evangelization

Missionaries came to Africa with a two-fold purpose: "to bring the heathen peoples individually to the fold of salvation, and uplifting them from primitivity to civilization."[4] Africans were seen as people with "empty heads and uncommitted souls."[5] Such impressions made Africa a "fertile" mission field where every seed whether it be theological, ideological, or cultural, germinates and flourishes freely. In the past, missionary "friends" represented everything from think-tank to "coin-tank" (i.e., they either tried to attract us with ideas or money). Although paternalistic, most mission projects were holistic in their perspective and approach.

The Present of Christian Evangelization

In the post-independent Africa (since the 1960s), missions have tended to shift their attention and efforts to the "winning of souls" as their primary duty. The shift of attention and efforts has created some tensions due to lack of identity with the society in which the gospel is preached. Mugambi has observed that this tension is the result of what he describes as "the crisis of credibility which the churches may have created because of failing to identify themselves convincingly with the national aspirations of the young African nations"[6]

In Africa today, the questions are: "How does the church remain the light and salt in a decaying society, where the future of the youth looks bleak, the eyes of the sick in hospitals proclaim hopelessness due to either lack of medicine or money to bribe medical personnel?" and "How does the church remain the light and salt for a continent where justice is in the pockets of "the haves," and people are homeless in their own land?

Alton B. Pollard has expressed the same concern in posing the question, "How does the Christian church affirm sacred truths in the midst of an inhospitable and, at times, outright hostile world?"[7] It has been noted in one of the "challenging essays in pastoral care" that, "Africans need to know Christ not only as Savior and Lord of souls but also giver of children, of plentiful harvest, of prosperity in trade, of success at work and also as one who has conquered all the forces that are inimical to persons total well-being."[8]

The gospel of salvation in Africa must reflect the African understanding of the terminology if at all it is going to elicit any response which is genuine and durable. A study done among the Annang people of Nigeria regarding salvation, which is rendered by the Annang word *edinyanga,* gives us some insight concerning the African concept of salvation. The six basic meanings of the word can be put into two categories.

Negatively *edinyanga* means the transference from the state of danger to a peril-free one; freedom from physical attack; and protection from whatever would inflict a jeopardy. Positively *edinyanga* means an increase and progress in the state that is conceived as safe, prosperous, or glorious; maintenance of a peaceful relationship with the objects and persons on which and whom one's own harmony and that of the world around one depend; and any action that brings about *edinyanga*.

The six meanings of *edinyanga* noted above correspond very closely to the meanings of a Swahili word for salvation, *wokovu.* For the word and act of salvation to make sense to an African, it must be presented and applied to the holistic context of life. According to Norman E. Thomas, new African religious movements draw more members because they feel a need to be protected against life's undesirable circumstances and believe with all their hearts that they will find such protection in the new movements.[9]

The Future of Christian Evangelization

The church must be forever building, for it is forever decaying within and attacked from without.[10] This idea from T. S. Eliot, quoted by Pollard, shows that the work of building the church is infinite. The mistakes of our "friends" in the past, and our struggles of today, should prepare the church to face the future more confidently.

The church should work toward nurturing a holistic growth patterned after the incarnate Christ who grew in wisdom, stature and favor with God (Luke 2.52). To achieve holistic growth, the church must proclaim a true and total gospel aimed at a total person for total transformation. As Christians, it is necessary that we affirm in words and deeds the United Nations Charter which states "the determination of its members to reaffirm faith in fundamental human rights in the dignity and worth of the human person."[11]

Theological education in Africa could help those preaching the gospel to be more contextual and relevant in three ways. First, our theological education programs should include in their curricula courses that affirm the dignity and worth of every African. The "bulldozer mentality"[12] of western missionaries, which seeks to uproot everything African in order to make clean room for reconstruction by using western design and materials, should be rejected.

Secondly, new missionaries from the West coming to Africa need to attend orientation programs conducted in a local seminary setting to give them the opportunity to reshape their mission perceptions and to be able to contextualize the gospel. Such programs should be conducted by Africans.

Thirdly, theological training programs in Africa need to prepare Africans for missions both inside and outside of Africa. This will help to neutralize cultural infiltration caused by one culture dominating mission enterprise, by providing qualified nationals who can preach the gospel in a more contextual way with less risk of acculturation.

NOTES

[1]All Africa Churches Conference, *Africa in Transition: The Challenge and the Christian Response* (Geneva: Word Council of Churches, n.d.), 11.

[2]J.K.N. Mugambi, *From Liberation to Reconstruction: African Christian Theology After the Cold War* (Nairobi East Africa Educational Publishers 1995), 26.

[3]A. Nasimiya-Wasike and Douglas W. Waruta, eds., *Mission in African Christianity: Critical Essays in Missiology* (Nairobi: Uzima Press, 1993), 141.

[4]J.K.N. Mugambi, *African Heritage and Contemporary Christianity* (Nairobi: Longman Kenya 1989), 39.

[5]Ibid., 22.

[6]Ibid., 24.

[7]Alton B. Pollard III, "When World Views Collide: Religion and the Culture of Disbelief," *Theology Today* 51:4 (January 1995), 583.

[8]Douglas Waruta and H.W. Kinoti eds., *Pastoral Care in African Christianity: Challenging Essays in Pastoral Theology* (Nairobi: Action Press, 1994), 22.

[9]Norman E. Thomas, "Images of Church and Mission in African Independent Churches," *Missiology: An International Review* 23:1 (January 1995), 20.

[10]Cited by Pollard, 583.

[11]Lutheran World Federation, LWF Documentation 35 (September 1994), 96.

[12]A. Nasimiyu-Wasike and Douglas W. Waruta, 143.

A Gospel for Nigerians

Osadolor Imasogie

Africa is a large continent covering about 11,960,000 square miles and inhabited by approximately two thousand ethnic groups speaking in the neighborhood of 800 distinct languages, not counting the various dialects spoken by sub-ethnic groups. The inhabitants of Africa are as diverse in physical features as they are in cultures, religions and languages. For those reasons alone it seems presumptuous for one person to claim to be speaking for Africa. Therefore, I have modified slightly the theme of our conference by entitling my paper "A Gospel for Nigerians."

I do not mean to deny the similarities of African cultures and worldviews in general terms. There is such a thing as "Africanness" running through our experiences and perception. We must, however, not forget that there are peculiarities that should not be ignored, and that demand caution in our claim to speak for Africa, as if it is one homogeneous family.

What is the Gospel of Christ?

I found it necessary to examine the meaning of the gospel before looking at it from the African point of view. Deep down in the inner recesses of the center of every person's being there is a sense of a void, a feeling of alienation from the source of one's being. It does not matter whether the feeling of alienation is expressed consciously, it is the story of every one who dares to probe the seat of self-consciousness. The sense of alienation has no respect for the color of one's skin or one's geographical location, although the search for a solution to the sense of alienation will inevitably be affected by culture.

The Bible teaches that the only authentic remedy for the gnawing sense of alienation lies in the gospel:

> God's power to save all who believe, first, the Jews and also the Gentiles. For the gospel reveals how God puts people right with himself. It is through faith from beginning to the end. As the scripture says: The person who is put right with God through faith shall live (Rom 1.16-17).

For Africans, the gospel ideally would mean all that is implied in the Pauline understanding cited above. Spelled out in plain words, the gospel means reconciliation to God, who is the Creator, through divine initiative, resulting in our gracious incorporation into God's life. Reconciliation is made possible by whole-hearted repentance of sin, and acceptance of the Christ-event as God's gracious approach to humanity.

There are various experiential implications of an authentic understanding of the gospel. First, the gospel means a full restoration to spiritual union with God, thus ensuring the ultimate consummation of eternal life, a foretaste of which is marked by the indwelling Spirit of God. Africans expect to experience the indwelling of God's spirit and a future eternal life. Next, the restored relationship also guarantees victory over sin. Sin is defeated in all its various manifestations, including death and the demonic forces we encounter in our earthly pilgrimage. The gospel means that because God has reconciled us, we have an obligation—as aided by the Holy Spirit—to be reconciled to our fellow humanity. The validity of the new status with God, brought about by grace, demands that the African Christians see themselves as ambassadors of Christ through whom Christ continues the ministry of reconciliation and transformation of the world to conform with God's purpose in creation (2 Cor 5.16-21). The presence of the Holy Spirit is the earnest of what is to come, and the experience of the Spirit makes Christians yearn for the time when both we and nature will be transformed, and God will make "us his sons and set our whole being free from decay to share the glorious freedom of the children of God" (Rom 8.18-25ff.).

Has the Gospel so Understood
Found Adequate Articulation in Africa?

My description of what the gospel—given above—means to us in Africa is predicated by the word ideally. The adverb is used deliberately to suggest that, by and large, the presentation of the gospel, especially among mainline churches, has not given adequate emphasis to a full meaning of the gospel. Therefore, the practical proclamation of the gospel has not enabled the average African to appropriate the gospel as the all-sufficient divine provision for humanity here and for eternity. The lack of an adequate articulation of the gospel has resulted in the inability of many believers to embrace Christ as the all sufficient Savior described in the New Testament. As I have stated elsewhere:

> The truth of this assertion is borne out by the fact that in times of existential crisis, many respectable African Christians revert to traditional religious practices as a means for meeting spiritual needs.[1]

The reason for this unfortunate reaction—reverting to traditional religion—of average African Christians in times of boundary situation crises lies in the failure of the mainline churches to proclaim the gospel in its fullness. Foreign missionaries, and those pastors trained by them, fail to give serious consideration to the total worldview of the African as part of an authentic presentation of the gospel. The unintended implication is that the gospel is presented as a foreign religion planted on a foreign soil.

There is no intention in what is said above to cast any aspersion on the foreign missionaries who risked life and property to carry the gospel to Africa. From all indications, the missionaries acted from good motives as committed servants of Christ. In other words:

> Motivated by a legitimate zeal to Christianize the world, these missionaries came to Africa with the conviction that their understanding of God as revealed in Christ had an identical universal application in all human situations and conditions irrespective of different world-views, self-understanding and consequent cultural expressions of religious experience [of any particular people].[2]

In their conviction about the universality of their theology, the missionaries forgot that their theology, like any other theological formulation, was a contextualized apprehension of the meaning of the gospel for them as filtered through their world-view and their self-understanding.

Any theology that ignores the world-view and self-understanding nurtured in its original setting can not adequately meet the deepest needs of a people in a different setting. Truth is one and absolute, but it can only be understood through the perceptive apparatus provided by one's world-view. I mean to emphasize that human perception of God is usually passed through the prism of the cultural influences that shaped human self-understanding and concomitant perceived needs. This is what Charles Kraft means in saying that

> [I]n an absolute sense, reality and truth remain one. But...it is a fact of life that perceptions of that reality and truth differ greatly from culture to culture...even from individual to individual within a given culture.[3]

There is no question that the purpose of the proclamation of the gospel is to show people that God, in a decisive act in Jesus Christ of Nazareth, has made eternal and sufficient provision for human salvation in its fullness. The point is that the proclaimer's knowledge of the self-understanding of a particular people is necessary to present the gospel through a language and meaningful symbols that will enable hearers of the gospel to have an effective apprehension and appropriation of how the gospel addresses their lives.

How Can the Gospel Best Meet the Needs of the People of Africa?

From the foregoing description of the apparent inability of the average African to accept the all-sufficiency of Christ it becomes imperative to seek ways of contextualizing the gospel. I have already argued that any theological formulation that is to be relevant is one that is not carried out in a vacuum. Theologizing is not an easy task; it calls for the best efforts of those who proclaim the gospel. They must be spiritually sensitive to the presence of God as they seek to interpret temporal realities in the light of God's self-disclosure, which by its very spiritual nature does not come in black and white.

Similar to miners of precious mineral, embedded deep down in the rocks, interpreters of the gospel must be armed with a clear understanding of the worldview of their target group, and be intently atuned to God's spirit as they enter the quarry of God's word. They should come to the task with prayer, and with the understanding that God speaks to humanity through the constructs of their worldviews and thought patterns. Our Lord, as the master teacher, exemplified the principle of listening and interpretation in his teaching. He was immersed in the world and culture of his people, and utilized the worldview and communication symbols which he and they shared in common. In context Jesus masterly communicated the eternal truth of God in a form that his contemporaries could understand.

The example of the manner of the teaching of Jesus is the hallmark of contextualization which every theologian will do well to keep constantly in mind, especially when seeking to present the gospel in a different culture. The thought provoking observation of Jürgen Moltmann is very enlightening here:

> The theologian is a strange creature, he is obliged to talk about God who is unconditionally present to all men in all times and all places but he is himself only a man who is limited in his capacities and who is conditioned in his views by his own tradition and culture...As I am not an angel but only a man, my perspectives are very limited. They are European and white, protestant and middle class, out of the twentieth century (I hope) and are ultimately determined by my personal experiences and private limitations. They have, therefore, only limited value and can only suggest to other theologians from other lands and churches and cultures that they look in the same direction from their points of view toward the God who has brought us into this community and who will bring us to a better community.[4]

A serious commitment to contextualization must be informed by the truth expressed by Moltmann. The reason is that theology that is relevant to a people must be one incarnated in their culture, language, thought patterns and symbols of communication, without which their total needs can not be adequately satisfied. After all, does the Bible not tell us that the eternal word became flesh, and dwelled among us to enable us perceive his glory as the glory of the only begotten Son who is full of grace and truth? (John 1.14).

The failure of the mainline churches in Africa to pay adequate attention to contextualization has produced many superficial Christians who only give intellectual assent to the truth of the gospel. Superficiality exists because no serious account was taken of the worldview and self-understanding. For instance, and African worldview has room for Satan and his demonic attacks, but the gospel as presented in mainline churches regards Satan and demons as superstition which are not expected to be believed by a "modern" person. As a result, when the average African Christian has a spiritual problem that is perceived as a demonic attack, help is sought from traditional religionists who handle the problem with traditional African methods. The underlying conviction is that the "White Man's God" does not know any thing about demonic attack.

Another example is the way the African worldview lays emphasis on the inner-penetration between the invisible and visible dimensions of existence, which enables ancestral spirits and deities to exert significant influences for good and ill on human beings. The African, therefore, constantly seeks protection and guidance from spiritual realities through the occultic expertise of the medicine men and diviners. In principle, there is similarity between the African world-view and the biblical world view. Mainline church theology, however, tends to regard the African perspective as superstition, rather than addressing it with Hebrews 4.13, which emphasizes that we live in the presence of the omnipresent God before whom all creatures remain naked. As a result of the failure of the church to consider the impact of a belief in the influence of spirits, many ancestral African Christians have no qualms about certain moral sins which they would have been afraid to commit before becoming a Christian because of fear of the divinities and ancestral spirits who uphold accepted moral standard.

An African worldview also places much emphasis on blood sacrifices as atonement for sin. Despite the fact that this is also a biblical emphasis, the perceived "modern" aesthetic value seems to make the mainline church theologian play down the significance of blood atonement. These are a few samples of elements of an African worldview that the church failed to take into account in its theological formulation. The result is a reinforcing of the wrong notion that Christianity is a foreign religion.

The notion of Christianity as a foreign religion prevailed until recently, when the Independent—or better still "Protest"—African Church movements and then new Pentecostal churches took the initiative in contextualizing the gospel. Those groups here given an appropriate emphasis on, among other things, the blood of Jesus, the efficacy and meaning of his sacrificial death, his resurrection and the ongoing intercessory role at the throne of mercy. They also have focused attention on the guiding role of the Holy Spirit, the power in the name of Jesus, and the necessity of prayer in the life of a Christian whose aim is victorious living in all circumstances.

Despite some unorthodox practices, bordering on syncretism, of these new versions of the Christian church, no one can honestly deny the fact that their rightful cognizance of the place of African worldview in contextualization has brought a needed vitality and fuller commitment to the Christian faith in Africa. The empirical result is that nearly every street in Nigerian cities and villages is dotted with one Pentecostal church of one hue or the other. Consequently, the number of adherents to the Christian faith is rising phenomenally to the extent that some Christian Association of Nigeria, sources now put the national Christian community as constituting between 60% and 66% of the national population. Although there is no official national documentation of such statistics, it is a welcome increase from the 32% Nigerian Christians reported in a national census three decades ago. There is a rumor that the exclusion of one's religious identity from the personal data required in the recent national census is the government's attempt to conceal the fact that there are more Christians in Nigeria than Muslims.

Christianity has had positive impact on Nigeria through the years. In spite of what has been said about the past failure to contextualize, western educational institutions and health care delivery centers were provided by Christian Missions until the middle of seventies when the Nigerian government ostensibly assumed half-hearted responsibility for those social services. At the time of political independence, a lion's share of leadership positions were held by Christians, many of whom were nominal because of lack of contextualization as already stated.

I believe that a stronger and more positive impact could have been made on Nigerian society if contextualization of the gospel had begun earlier. There is a great hope for the future of the gospel in Nigeria, if concerted sound theological guidance is given to the ongoing process of contextualization.

NOTES

[1]Osadolor Imasogie, *Guidelines for Christian Theology in Africa* (Achimota, Ghana: African Christian Press, 1983), 23.

[2]Osadolor Imasogie, "African Theology: The Development of Theological Thought in Nigeria," *The Baptist Quarterly* (October 1992), 390.

[3]Charles Kraft, *Christianity in Culture*, 228.

[4]Jürgen Moltmann, "Christian Theology and Its Problems Today," *Reformed World* 32:1 (1972), 5.

The Whole Gospel
for a Changing South African World

Louise Kretzschmar

The gospel has brought great blessing to many in Africa
(although what accompanied it also often brought equally great suffering). Today the gospel presents us with the challenge of living out
the implications of salvation in a variety of contexts. Africa is a huge
continent composed of many different countries and containing
enormous natural and human resources. Nonetheless, because of the
colonial and neocolonial history of Africa, and as a result of many of
its present leaders, Africa remains a continent of enormous need. A
central challenge to Africans is how to develop our rich resourses—
both natural and human—and how to use those resourses in a sustain-
able manner that may benefit the whole continent.

While South Africa shares many of the cultural loyalties and
some of the problems prevalent throughout the rest of the continent,
South Africa also is different. White domination has a much longer
history in South Africa, particularly in the form of Apartheid. Also,
unlike other African countries, several million white South Africans
settled here generations ago; their descendants have both benefitted
from the country, and contributed significantly to its development.

Within the African context, the process of the Africanization,
which involves relating the gospel to the different contexts across
Africa, needs further exploration and development. Many of the
strengths of African culture, such as an emphasis on community and
holistic approachs to life (rather than limiting "religion" to a narrow
area of life), must be further incorporated into our theology, and our
activities in our churches. African Christians (i.e., those Christians
who were born in, or are committed to, Africa) need to take the lead
in Africanization. We must ask: What aspects of our changing cul-

tures are compatible (or incompatible) with the gospel of Jesus Christ? What aspects of our cultures can be incorporated into our faith? Which features should be completely discarded? Which gospel expressions ought to be transformed?

All theology is contextual because it reflects the setting within which it is written. The issue, therefore, is not whether our theology is contextual or not, but whose context is being reflected. The so-called "contextual theologies," such as African, liberation or feminist theology, differ from traditional theologies only in that they deliberately seek to address contexts and perceptions that previously have been largely ignored. Until this generation, what has been called "theology" could be more accurately described as North American, German, or English theology. Equally apt, but more controversial, dominant theology before the 1970s could be termed white, clerical, male, and ruling or middle class theology.

As important as contextuality is, especially in terms of the need to relate the gospel to actual situations that pertain in African contexts, it should never deteriorate into mere relativism. Baptists in South Africa need to have meaningful contact with a range of other Christian groups, both within and without the historic Baptist tradition, so that we can be challenged by the critiques, visions and achievements of our sisters and brothers in Christ who have a different heritage.

If we believe that Christ can meet our needs, and equip us to face challenges, we must begin by identifying what these needs and challenges are. The church in South Africa faces a variety of challenges. Below I will explore challenges that face individuals, families, and larger societies.

Over several centuries many Africans have come to faith in Jesus Christ, and they have sought to live out their faith in practical ways. As a result of the gospel, many churches have been established; the power of the gospel has also led to the establishment of a number of schools, hospitals, and other institutions. The gospel has brought forgiveness, faith, salvation, and healing (in the broadest sense of the term) to many millions of people in Africa. The contemporary challenge for the churches in South Africa is to continue to proclaim the personal salvation that is to be found in Christ. The gospel at least means that people should continue to come to faith in Christ, and to experience the growth, healing, and empowerment that Christ brings to individuals. We need to be delivered from our sins, fears, and pain; we need to become whole and mature persons through the power of the gospel.

The gospel does not end at the personal level. While it is true that persons need to experience redemption and begin to learn to be Christ's disciples, discipleship also needs to be lived out in all the facets of their lives.

Families and local communities in South Africa are in need of Christ as much as are individuals. The results of separation, poverty, brokenness, abuse, indifference, conflict—and also the deliberate infliction of pain—are widely manifest. Our churches must not fail to see the results of sin, and seek to bring the power of the gospel into these contexts. Christ came to save sinners; Christians cannot turn their backs on those who are trapped by their own sins, or are suffering as a consequence of the personal or structural evil of others. Further, the church needs to put its own house in order by assisting its own members to overcome their experiences of bondage or failure so that they can be enabled to be of service to others.

Following recent political developments, South Africans are faced with enormous social challenges. Government, the law, the economy, education, the police force, and public services all need to be restructured. Further, racial reconciliation and the development of new power relations between black and white South Africans needs to continue. There is also an enormous need for a process of reconstruction and development to be initiated and maintained. All of the noted challenges will involve, among other things, the supply of housing, land, services, hospitals and employment to those who have previously been ignored and oppressed.

Clearly, none of our social challenges can be achieved easily. Conflicts have, and will, arise between the various role players. The essential task is to seek to preserve what is right and to change what is wrong in such a way that people actually experience the benefits of change. The government of National Unity cannot afford to alienate its educated and prosperous citizens, because it needs them to assist in the goal of reconstruction. Equally, the government needs to satisfy the needs of the previously-marginalized citizens in such a way that the economy grows rather than stagnates. In all efforts to meet the social challenge, justice and compassion need to be central. If justice and compassion are not central, the evils of the past will be repeated in different forms.

The churches can play an important role in social change because they have direct access to some of the key leaders in the various sectors of our society. The churches are also home to many of the ordinary persons who will be needed to actually put new policies into practice. If the Christian churches are to have a meaningful and lasting impact upon South Africa as a whole, deliberate strategies need to be devised and implemented.

Christians need to seek to fully and continuously experience the grace and power of God in their own lives, and in their churches. Only a deep and continuing experience of God will effectively energize us to face the tasks ahead. Our experience of the salvation that Christ brings in every area of our lives, and our participation in the fellowship of believers, is what will enable us to preach to and serve those around us.

Secondly, churches need to identify the particular gifts and callings of their members, and support them in their involvement in the variety of areas mentioned above. In all efforts toward reconstruction Christians can act as the proverbial "salt" and "light" in our broken, suffering, and rebellious world. In the attempt to build a genuinely "new" South Africa, the church needs both to set an example and prophetically to proclaim the need for the values of competence and commitment, integrity, justice, and demonstrate an empowering compassion for the poor that will be visible in our society.

Thirdly, the churches need to affirm the voice of the voiceless and not permit those in power to grasp everything for themselves. Black Christians, who are moving up the social and economic ladder, need to be challenged to make available their resources and skills. White Christians, too, need to be assisted to come to terms with the many bewildering changes taking place on a daily basis. All South African Christians need genuinely to repent of the sins of the past and to be challenged to contribute their energies and resources to the building of a country that reflects both personal and social morality.

The gospel is the "good news" that salvation, which involves repentance, forgiveness, healing, new life, and empowerment by the Holy Spirit, can be received from the hand of Christ. In Africa as a whole, and especially in South Africa, the challenge of the gospel is for believers to review what we believe the gospel teaches, and to actually live it out in our personal, family, and social lives. We need to avoid the dualism, individualism and lack of contextual awareness that has characterized so much of our (imported) theology, the activities of our churches, and the vision of our members.

The challenge throughout Africa is for the church, both as a community, and as individual Christians in their personal capacity, to experience, preach and actively initiate the gospel values of forgiveness, healing, reconciliation, justice, compassion, and integrity within the context of our vast continent. Such a vision is in line with the Baptist Convention's emphasis on a holistic, Afrocentric, and participatory Christian gospel.

Part Two
Accents from Asia

A Gospel of Christ, *Not* Christianity

Wati Aier

The postcolonial era in most Asian nations was primarily founded on economic and social development. Socioeconomic development brings with it political and theological implications. The gap between the rich and the poor, and the suppression of human rights and freedom of expression call for more than socioeconomic reflections. On the theological front in the 1990s, (as opposed to the decades of the 1960s and 1970s, when Asian Christians and churches were mostly dependent on western Christian leadership), there has been a shift toward more reliance upon local and indigenous leadership. The shift has also given rise to a greater acceptance of a distinctly Asian community of Christians.

With these developments a number of theologies have crowded onto the Asian soil, often under the theological rubric of "contextualization." The term "contextualization" was coined by the adherents of the Theological Education Fund in the early 1970s, to identify evolving theological methodologies found in given historical and social contexts.[1] In its formative period the term was defined:

> Contextualization is not simply a fad or catch-word but a theological necessity demanded by the incarnational nature of the Word. What does the term imply? It means all that is implied in the familiar term "indigenisation" and yet seeks to press beyond. Contextualization has to do with how we assess the peculiarity of Third World contexts. Indigenisation tends to be used in the sense of responding to the gospel in terms of a traditional culture...Contextualization, while not ignoring this, takes into account the process of secularity, technology, and the struggle for human justice, which characterize the historical movement of nations in the Third World.[2]

Based upon this broad definition, contextualization has been employed for various theological models, sometimes leading to syncretistic and accommodative tendencies. Abuses of the idea of contextualization does not negate the fact that the proclamation of the gospel must be authentically and meaningfully communicated within one's own cultural context. If theological reflection describes faith within a particular cultural context—as it always does—then it is at least a contextual discipline. The proclamation of the gospel is intrinsically connected to the particular social and cultural contexts where faith is nurtured and explored.

Affirming the need for contextualization of the gospel poses certain questions: What is the central message of the gospel? What is the foundation or the premise of the proclamation? How should the gospel be proclaimed, making Christ and his claims authentic among the peoples and cultures in Asia than the authority of secularism? Who is Jesus Christ in relation to other faiths?

Contextualization: Claim and Meaning of the Gospel

The danger of Asian Christians fighting against oppression and suffering on political and social fronts is that our theology and lives are a close reflection of the struggle. We risk being co-opted by the values of the sociopolitical struggles that have entered our world from the West. What good is the contextualization of the "secular city," if it is found to be without foundations upon which to build?

A theology that affirms that in Christ God became secular or worldly—following the western import of Harvey Cox's ideas that theology has come to celebrate the realization of biblical motifs in its technology, and nobility of the secular city is not adequate to the demands to proclaim an authentic gospel. Because of the fallenness of the creation, many Asian Christians are becoming increasingly aware that the world cannot be accepted as it is. At the center of the secular city is its greed, blight, and alienation. The same observation can be applied to societies throughout ages.

Secular theology, as affirmed by some, contends that the world is the object of God's love and, therefore, demands that we must also love the world. If we genuinely are to love the world, we cannot love it as it is. We must go beyond secularism. As Christians, we must love the world so much that we want it to become what God intends it to be, the new creation promised in Jesus Christ. We must also love humanity so much that we want it to become transformed through Christ.

The claim and the meaning of the gospel is that in Jesus Christ the cycle of moral and spiritual death has been broken. Accommodation, complicity and compromise with the secular world may be the attitude of some contextual theologies, but the gospel is in conflict with such a position. In making theological confessions rooted in realism, reasonableness, and respectability, the gospel includes the possibility of persecution, God-forsakenness, and crucifixion seeking first the kingdom. As Moltmann says: "If Christians are to know for what reasons they are here, they must also rediscover who they really are."[3]

If we are serious enough, Asian church leaders must resist the temptation to reduce the claims of Christ by negotiating and softening the demands of the gospel. A half-century ago, Richard Niebuhr commented: "A God without wrath brought man without sin into a kingdom without judgment through the ministrations of a Christ without a cross."[4] Niebuhr's caricature of the Social gospel represents the mood of a generation reacting against the false optimism of the values of humanism. The Social gospel Movement reduced the advent of the kingdom of to a secular doctrine of progress, along with its high estimate of human nature. This generation of Asian Christians is faced with a similar threat that the gospel will be reduced to a mere movement.

Lacking strong bases for optimism in the activity of man and woman, Christians base their optimism on a Christocentric faith. Such faith, however, should not imply a mood of resignation that leaves everything to God. Rather, it sees the breaking in of God's future— the kingdom of God—as an explosive and liberating power that can elicit a radical and revolutionary response from men and women.

In our own time and context, disillusionment with faith that is falsely optimistic about humanity and social programs should lead us to rediscover the biblical doctrine of alienation. Because the fundamental problem of our age is to be found in men and women, the solution could not be found exclusively in human efforts, but beyond—in

God's revelation and activity through Christianity. If society with its false priorities, its classicism, and its militarism is basically sick, then salvation will not come either through natural evolution (the hope of liberalism) or through penetration of structures by Christian action and programs (the hope of secular theology). Something else is needed. Asian Christians need the vision of God pulling people together to live in the real and new age. We are people who need to feel liberated from the corrupt institutions of the present age.

Since the radical Christians do not believe in relinquishing the responsibility to participate in God's redeeming activity in the world, they are searching for new paradigms for the Christian life; they are, testing new strategies for Christian living; and they are open to new forms of Christian witness and action. Without a clear understanding of the meaning of a personal encounter with Christ, theological tasks become absurd or merely matters of academic debate.

Asian church leaders also must reflect seriously on Christianity that fosters an acceptance of the cultural and political status quo. Such brands of Christianity quickly proclaim Jesus as Savior, but often in ways that obscure implications of his lordship over all of life. At best such expressions of faith are spiritualized into irrelevance, as Jim Wallis claims: "The influence of individualism and the ethic of success in evangelism has resulted in a depreciation of Jesus' call for public ministry."[5]

The heresy of grace without discipleship (as articulated by Dietrich Bonhoffer) has come to characterize the proclamations of so-called conservative Christianity. The emphasis on the privatistic notion of salvation has separated itself from the social and political meaning and responsibility of loving the world enough to want it to become the kind of world God intends it to be. The Bible clearly points out that personal faith divorced from an active commitment to social justice is a mockery of the gospel. Paul describes the cosmic and political implications of the resurrected Lord who has won the victory over the fallen powers and principalities of the world systems that hold people captive, thus breaking their absolute dominion and assuring their final defeat (Eph 6.10-17).

We must recognize that God's revelation will never be congenial to the presuppositions of secular society and culture. The last thing that the competing religions and political factions of the first century wanted was to accept Jesus of Nazareth and his gospel of the Kingdom of God. A faithful proclamation of the gospel in every age and setting will most often risk similar offensive and disruptive qualities. The authentic gospel must not be distorted or redefined in order to make it more acceptable to the dominant cultural, religious, intellectual and political consensus of any place or time.

Contextualization: Jesus Christ vis-à-vis Other Faiths

In the midst of diverse religious beliefs and faiths, the theologies of contextualization have been readily employed by Asian theologians. For instance, M. M. Thomas has theologized the concept of salvation in terms of humanization: "I cannot see any difference between the accepted goal of a Christian church expressing Christ in terms of a contemporary Hindu concept and life patterns and a Christ-centered Hindu church in Christ which transforms Hindu thought and life patterns within."[6]

Following the theological route of M. M. Thomas, several younger theologians in Asia have emerged. A fine example is C. S. Song:

> It is no longer simply a question of evangelizing the so-called non-Christians....It is important here for us to ask: From the Christian point of view, how can Christian spirituality and Asian spirituality intersect in such a way that people begin to see the historical meaning of their existence in their new light?[7]

There is a need for addressing the gospel in the context of a pluralistic society. While there may be the so-called Indian theology, Japanese theology, Korean theology and so on, they are only authentically Christians when they stem from biblical understandings that confess that there must be universally valid truths. That is, the Christ relevant to people in America also must be relevant to people in India, Korea, Japan, or else we will be in the business of proclaiming a chameleon theology that has no true color, but changes from one context to another context.

It is true that, to a large extent, Christianity's attitude to other religions has been shaped by the colonial mentality, as John Stott notes:

> [I]t is certainly embarrassing for us in West to have to acknowledge that during those centuries of colonial expansion, territorial and spiritual conquest, politics and religion, gun and Bible, the flag and the cross, went hand and hand, and that representatives of the imperial power often developed attitudes of proud superiority towards those they ruled...But the Christian missionary enterprise, in seeking to win to Christ adherents of other religions, is not in itself a mark of arrogance; it indicates rather a profound and humble conviction that the gospel is superior to other faiths because it is God's revealed truth.[8]

The colonial mentality of Christianity in Asia has given rise to indigenous and contextual theologies, that often reacted, against western theologies, rather than being informed by them. One cannot ignore this aspect of Asian theology while talking of contextualization. Among Asian theologians there has been varied reactions to the western brand of theologies. There is a danger, however, of being diverted from biblical truths for the sake of reaction. After being trained in the West, I have often found myself taking on a radical position in this regard, only to find that again and again, that there is a vast difference between intellectual theologizing and the praxeological dimension of the gospel. Unlike the theologian of the West, here in Asia a theological teacher is often a pastor, evangelist and a counselor. Very often he/she is asked to preach in evangelistic gatherings, and lead seminars on social and political issues. In such situations, the questions are: What is our message? What do we have to offer that other disciplines cannot? Who is Jesus Christ in relation to varied forms of religious beliefs?

It is to be noted that Christians claim uniqueness only for Christ and not Christianity in many of its forms or cultural situations. "The uniqueness of Christianity is in Jesus Christ."[9] Following this premise, Asian Christian leaders can humbly enter into a meaningful interaction with other religions without falling into inclusivism or pluralism, that is, neither allowing our theology to claim that salvation is possible to adherents of other faiths, or to simply accept that all religions are equal thereby disclaiming the uniqueness of Jesus Christ.

A Christian's dialogue with another implies neither a denial of the uniqueness of Christ, nor any loss of one's commitment to Christ, but rather that a genuinely Christian approach to others must be human, personal, relevant and humble. In dialogue we share our common humanity, its dignity and its fallenness, and express our common concern for that humanity.[10]

Our goal as Asian Christians is to awaken faith under the lordship of Christ. In the dialogue with other religions, we do not lose our identity, but have the possibility of emerging from the dialogues with new profiles. It may be said that these profiles will be turned towards abolition of prejudices about other faiths, and be passionate about others suffering and justice and their future, towards full life in Christ.

NOTES

[1]David J. Bosch, *Transforming Mission: paradigm shifts in theology of mission* (Maryknoll, New York: Orbis, 1991), 420 ff.
[2]As quoted by Bon Rin Ro, ed., *Ministry in Context* (Bromley, England: Theological Education Fund, 1972), 64.
[3]Jürgen Moltmann, *Religion, Revolution and the Future* (New York: Scribners, 1969), 134.
[4]H. Richard Niebuhr, *The Kingdom of God in America* (Philadelphia: Westminster Press,), 193.
[5]Jim Wallis, *Agenda For Biblical People* (San Francisco: Harper and Row, 1984), 47.
[6]M. M. Thomas, *Salvation and Humanization*, 40.
[7]C. S. Song, *Third Eye Theology* (Maryknoll: Orbis, 1979), 28.
[8]John R. W. Stott, *Christian Mission and the Modern World* (Downer's Grove, Illinois: InterVarsity Press, 1975), 300–301.
[9]John Mbiti, *African Religions and Philosophy* (Garden City, New York: Anchor Books, 1970), 277.
[10] Uppsala Statement, Report II (as quoted by Stott, 71).

An Indian Gospel for India

O. M. Rao

Since independence in 1947, the church in India has been engaged in the task of making the gospel relevant. The Christian church in India is closely linked to the imperial reign of Britain, and in many ways, with the rest of the West. The relationship carries two negative observations. When citizens with nationalistic fervor rose against British domination, the church found itself at a loss because the people who brought the gospel were under attack. For many Indians the most important question of the day was, "Are the Christians of India also patriots?"

The second observation concerns the ways the church adapted to the West. The manner of dress, the tunes of hymns sung in churches, the style of worship, and the type of theological training all resembled a culture that was strange to local people. Those western features of the gospel were tolerable at the early stages of the growth, because they had been introduced by western messengers who did what was customary in their home countries. In India today, however, western features of the celebration and practice of Christianity are not as tolerable.

Any talk of the "indigeninzation" or "contextualization" of the gospel in a larger setting must begin with the talk about redeeming the church, with all its accretions, from what I term "the Babylonian captivity of the West." What has been handed over by the westerners has been perpetuated until today, but in the subconscious mind of every Christian in India what happens in the church is nonetheless often quite foreign to the lives they live beyond Christian circles.

We can appreciate that the western missionaries did what they could under very hostile conditions, when they brought the gospel to Asia. Today it is left to nationals to bring about necessary changes. Contemporary Christians in India face a situation that is similar to that of Martin Luther, and his struggle against the Roman Catholic Church. In Luther's day the forces of the Roman Church were even more powerful than that of the secular powers. Protestantism would never have emerged, had it not been for God's providence. In India today the powers of a colonial past press hard upon us in the church, as well as outside.

A tragic fact of the history of the church in India is that the gospel that came to us from the East, through Syrian and Nestorian churches in the fifth century (or even earlier to Kerala) remained the prerogative of an exclusive group. The earliest Christians in India appeared similar to the Jews of the Diaspora of the region, who never carried their expression of faith to others in the country. If those first Christians in India had shared the gospel with others, perhaps a majority of contemporary Indians would have been in a church with an eastern flavor. Such a church would have been, perhaps, like the Moguls, under whom Islam spread. The Moguls never looked back to Afghanistan and Turkey, the countries of their Islamic origins. Instead they adapted themselves to the Indian situation, while at the same time maintaining their religious identity.[1]

When the missionaries came to India from the West, they did not intend to become acquainted with the culture of the people. They only had come to proclaim the gospel. These missionaries were more inclined to convert the heathen, as Indians were taken to be, rather than understand a culture. For that reason, anything that did not conform to western Christianity was considered pagan and, therefore, was rejected. Missionaries from the West did not participate in Indian community life, and they also encouraged converts to abandon it. New converts even were often placed in protective Christian compounds.

Western individualism—including the idea that beliefs are personal and do not change one's participation in the larger community—created difficulties for converts to Christianity. When the schedule castes were converted, it was largely on a village community level. In the case of caste hindus, however, conversion was an individual matter that, in turn, disrupted the convert's community. Converts from the social castes were dislodged from their society because the rigid caste system would not allow movement from one level to another. As a result, unless converts in a particular church were from the same caste, they would have difficulty living together. The consequences of this difficulty is the continuing existence of a caste system within church today, especially in the southern part of India.

Another example of difficulties arising from a refusal to appreciate local culture surrounds the eating of beef. The Hindu community looks down on beef eating because the cow is considered sacred. In the past cattle were useful for agricultural and economic reasons and were used as barter. Under the sacrificial system of the Rig Veda era, the flesh of cattle was commonly eaten by the Brahmins. Whatever the historical background, the present is quite different. Modern India is largely vegetarian, reflecting the influences of Buddhism.

Western missionaries, with their beef-eating backgrounds, could not follow Paul's instruction to abstain from meat if eating it offends the weaker brother or sister (Rom 14.20-21). The eating habits of Muslims stood as a great divide between the two large communities in India—Hindus and Muslims. When Christians arrived they added to the problem through their disregard for the dietary sentiments of the majority of Indians.

Another striking feature of the Asian church is the mixed-race population that has resulted from either the marriages between western rulers and local peoples, or the practice of western rulers keeping Indian mistresses (similar to what happens with the presence of military troops in a region). Children born of mixed unions would not be accepted into their caste, and would have to adopt the religion of their foreign parent, either Islam in the days of the Moguls, or Christianity during western rule.

Mixed-race children born during western rule usually carried western names. Often they adopted western habits of dress and eating, too. In some cases, genuine converts to Christianity also changed their names in order to identify with their new faith. Indians with western names seem a bit unnatural because in Indian culture a name often carries a distinct characteristic. For example, if a child born in a Andhra Pradosh dies in infancy, the next-born child is called *Pentayyah*, literally translated "garbage." If the child survives no one loathes such a name because it was given to ward off evil (because, according to the Tolugu culture, evil does not bother with garbage). The western names of Asians have no such cultural moorings, and often the third generation that has reintegrated into Indian culture hates the western names.

President General Mobuto of Zaire addressed a similar problem by issuing a governmental proclamation that all citizens of Zaire revert to their African names. And so it is in Zaire today. However strange the regional names such as Salt, Honey, and Dry Fish may sound to others, they carry deep cultural roots for Zairians.[2]

Is there a distinction between the classical Hinduism of India and the modern renascent cultures of Asia? In the early period, anything to be indigenous had to conform to classical Hinduism. For example, the incarnation of Jesus was often expressed indigenously with the Hindu term *avatar*. Classical Hinduism is being replaced in contemporary culture. In cities where various people from different cultures and styles of life come together, an amalgam of culture with modern and western tinges has come into vogue.

Today it is difficult to clearly distinguish what is Indian or Asian, although there are subtle examples in daily life. One example is the dress of the Indian woman: she does not abandon her sari. When the Roman Catholic Church brought its nuns and sisters to India, they wore the western frock, but when Mother Theresa (who is not an Indian) started the Sisters of Charity, she adapted the sari. Although she is known around the world for her service to down-trodden humanity, Mother Theresa chooses to identify with the local people; her dress is one indication of her local identification.

Men's dress is another example. Many men wear slacks instead of *dhotis*. One never sees a Hindu priest officiating while wearing a suit; neither do the worshipers wear western clothes. In the Christian churches, however, despite the sweltering Indian heat, our priests and pastors put on either cassocks or suits (or at least slacks with a shirt and tie). Why not adopt the type of dress Indians wear? It is adapted to the hot climate.

A final example from daily life is the use of music. All people love music. In our worship services music is an important way to sing praises to God. Why, then, do we sing English hymns with western tunes that are hardly sung outside the church? In many vernacular language churches the hymns are translated, but they are still sung to western tunes that have no relevance for our culture.

The pattern of theological education in our seminaries carries the old pattern of western training—the books are written by western church leaders, and the methods of teaching follow western examples.

An example is the discussion of Chalcedonian Christology, that is, the two natures in the Christ. In an Asian context the idea of the two natures of Christ will hardly be a problem because the culture accepts gods like Durga in Hinduism, who has six hands, or in Ramayana, and the Srilankan Ruler Ravana has ten heads. Such oddities are merely accepted as part of the religious faith found in Asia.

Many times theological studies follow the patterns of a religion department in a university. That approach often leads to higher critical study and what is seen as a liberal theological approach. The West can afford such an approach because its environment is predominantly Christian. In an Asian setting with a struggling church in a hostile environment, however, such an approach to theological training—worthwhile as it is—is a luxury, if not an anachronism. Ours in an environment that is largely religious, and we have to reckon with its different beliefs. Hinduism, with its tolerance based on Sanatana dharma, is willing to embrace Christ as one of the avatars. Many homes have images of Christ along with the gods such as Krishna, or Rama and the bhagawans, or the godman Sai Baba. The moment a Christian in such a context claims uniqueness for Christ, he or she is ostracized as being anti-national.

The Christological question needs to be examined within the religious context of Asia in general, and India in particular. The debate is based historically on Barthian fundamentalism. In the International Missionary Conference at Tambram, Madras, India in 1910, the Christological question became a crucial issue (as shown in Hendrik Kraemer's *The Christian Message in a Non-Christian World*[3]). Theologians such as Emil Brunner—and later Karl Rahner and Raimundo Panikkar (who is Asian)—held that God's revelation in the world, however dim, cannot be denied because God was active throughout history, even before Christ was revealed to the world. If that is so, religions other than Christianity must have some salient features that must be treated as God-given and, thus, must recognized and used for enriching the Christian faith. Of course features on the negative side that go against he will of God must be eschewed. The wholesale rejection of other religions as worthless has to be avoided, keeping in mind the uniqueness of Christ, which is central to the gospel. To lose the core of the gospel is to make our faith syncretistic. Such an issue may not be that much of a problem in the West, although they do have many religious cults and "isms," some of which are imported from the East.

Asia today becoming the theater of the Christian church in its active operation is largely a result of the missiological aspect of the church. Any theology of Asia should reckon with its distinctive mission involvement so that the major emphasis and orientation of all theological study is missions. We will either assert the lordship of Christ in the midst of hostile resurgent Asian religions, or we will succumb to their pressures to compromise with, if not being absorbed into, the pervading religious faiths that surround us.

Much of western thought does not speak to the Asian mind. We cannot help western writers, for example, in the Baptist World Alliance meetings, especially in our committee or commission gatherings. Papers read by westerns deal with issues raised and discussed in the West. When I read a paper from an Asian perspective, I find the western members of the audience are less knowledgeable than when I listen to a paper from a western perspective. Unfortunately the world body, including the Baptist World Alliance, revolves around western thought, and there is poor representation from Asia voices. It must be remembered that the arena of gospel challenge is in Asia today rather than the West. For that reason, attention and recognition should be given to Asian views.

It is not only a question of foreign elements in Christian faith and its unique claim, but also the disruption of the social structure made rigid by history. The fact that proclaimers of Christian faith show no regard for the cultural heritage of India alienates the church from the rest of society, or worse, makes society hostile toward Christian faith. In such situations the receptability of the gospel in Asia rates very low. It is true that with increasing modern culture, the national cultural barriers are coming down, yet the distinctive features of each culture are identifiable. Christians should be proud of their cultural heritage, and rely upon it to enrich the universal church with their distinctive cultures.

The Japanese characteristics trait provide an apt example for us. The Japanese first copied the western products, but then their serious research evolved products that today are distinctly Japanese. I apply this model to Asian church's theological context: we Asians have imitated the West long enough, and now it is time to bring out our national Asian Christian heritage to the Body of Christ. The success of the future of the church depends largely on this factor.

NOTES

[1] Jawaharlal Neru, *The Discovery of India* (London: Oxford University Press, 1946), 227ff.

[2] Taiye Aluke, "The Naming Ceremony in African Independent Churches," *The Indian Journal of Theology* (35, 1993), 20ff.

[3] Hendrik Kraemer, *The Christian Message in a Non-Christian World* (London: James Clark, 1947).

The Gospel in an Asian Incarnation

Renthy Kreitzar

The gospel of Jesus Christ has a universal message and is relevant in any context. Its original setting was the Hebrew culture but it transcended that world as it moved out of the Palestinian soil into Exile. We can see God preparing and transforming Hebrew culture as a medium of divine self-revelation in the person of Jesus Christ as confessed in the letter to the Hebrews: "but in these last days he has spoken to us by a Son, i.e. Jesus Christ, whom he appointed the heir of all things, through whom also he created the world" (1.2.). Thus we can say that God speaks to all people in all cultures and contexts.

The topic of this conference—a contextual approach to the gospel—raises an important point for the modern world. The biblical portrayal of the gospel is a paradigm that should offer insight. Contextualization may be seen throughout the biblical history, as God spoke to different people through the prophets (Heb 1.1). We also can recognize different theologies in the Old Testament, such as Yahwistic, Elohistic, Deuteronomic, Prophetic, Wisdom, and Priestly. Different theological interpretations in the New Testament are also evident, such as those found in Mark, Matthew, Luke, John, James, and Paul.

The theologies of the Old Testament were developed in different periods of Israel's history in the contexts of the socioreligious and contemporary realities of the people. For instance, the eras of nomadic movement and then the settlement of Canaan (ca. 1750–1050 B.C.E.) were the stage for the formation of Israelite traditions. These traditions were collected and appropriated in different intellectual centers during the periods of the monarchy and divided kingdoms of Israel and Judah (ca. 1050–586 B.C.E.). The Exile in Babylon eclipsed the faith of Judah for a while, only later to provide a platform for an enriched theology under the influence of the socioreligious cultures of Babylon and Persia. Doctrines common to Hellenistic Judaism such as universalism, angelology, and demonology, apocalypticism and messiansim, resurrection and eschatology developed during the exilic and postexilic periods.

Then Palestine came under the control of the Greek rulers (ca. 343 B.C.E.) making easy the ways of Hellenization, before giving way in New Testament times to Roman Rule (ca. 63 B.C.E.). Three distinct sociocultural contexts may be seen in the New Testament: the rural Palestine, the urban community of mixed population, and the Greco-Roman world. Almost all of the New Testament writings came from the third context. Only the sayings of Jesus were transmitted as *paradosis* (i.e., tradition). The New Testament writings presupposed such a transmission of *paradosis* (see, e.g., 1 Cor 15.1-3).

The "remembered" or "retold" accounts of the Jesus story as memoirs are preserved, in part, in the New Testament as Mark, Luke, Matthew, John, Acts, Paul's Letters, and so on. These writings were theological interpretations or appropriations of the teaching and sayings of Jesus in their cultural contexts. So we, the church, have received them as *paradosis* of the *kerygma* of Jesus, the gospel of Jesus.

Following the New Testament period, the subsequent periods also interpreted the paradosis of the kerygma in the contexts and cultures of different peoples down to modern times. And, therefore, in the history of the church throughout the ages theological formulations arose in the contexts of the sociocultural realities of the times. The creeds and confessions of the Patristic period were formulated as new theological statements in response to the cultural realities of different peoples, cultures and situations. Similarly, there has been an ongoing process of theologizing and theological formulation in the church from biblical times until today.

So we speak of patristic theology, biblical theology, Lutheran or Calvinistic theology of the Reformation, Thomistic theology, as well as the theology of Karl Barth, the theology of Paul Tillich, the theology of Jürgen Moltmann, the theology of M. M. Thomas, the theology of Kosuke Koyama, *minjung* theology, liberation theology, and, now, we even speak of new emerging theologies like feminist theology, *dalit* theology, tribal or indigenous theology.

We need not talk of the theology of a particular school or region, but we have to take into account the "various ways" that God speaks to different communities in the past, today and even in days to come. The gospel of Jesus Christ has an eternal message.

The message of the gospel came to Asia within the contexts of a plurality of political ideologies, cultures, and religions. When the gospel breaks in upon such contexts, similar to biblical situations in the past, it bears witness to the uniqueness of God's salvation in Jesus Christ (Acts 4.12). In this we recognize that God can speak to us today as Asians through Jesus Christ. That means, God can revive the power of the incarnation in every changing context, therefore making the gospel relevant. The revival of the incarnation is contextualization.

The content of the gospel message always remains the same, but presentation of it may vary in relevance from context to context. Hence, the gospel can be meaningful in the context of Hinduism, Buddhism, Islam, primal religion and culture, Confucianism, Shintoism, and the various political ideologies of Asian countries.

First, if we are serious about having meaningful dialogue with Hindus, and if we are committed to communicate the message of salvation in Jesus Christ to them, then we have to recognize that all humans are equal as created in God's own image, and therefore, have a commonality of humanity before God the creator, regardless of race, color, sex, or economic status. All humanity needs to turn to God in and through Jesus Christ as "the way, the truth, and the life" (John 14.6). Likewise, all people are united in the Body of Christ, and "there is neither bond nor free, male or female" (Gal 3.28). The different ways to God in Hinduism as *gnanamarga* ("way of knowledge"), *bhaktimarga* ("way of devotion or spirituality") and *karmamarga* ("way of religious duty") are indeed all summed up in Jesus Christ as "the way" (John 14.6; cf. Eph 1.9-10). And the believer may at last find *shanti* ("peace") in Jesus Christ as he himself says, "Peace I leave with you; my peace I give to you; not as the world gives do I give to you" (John 14.27; cf. 16.33; 20.19; Acts 10.36; Rom 5.1).

Secondly, similar to the above understanding of "peace" (*shanti*) in Hinduism, and its fulfillment that "peace" which God gives in Jesus Christ, according to Buddhism, there are four Noble Truths. (1) Suffering is a universal fact; (2) the cause of suffering is desire; (3) there is complete freedom from suffering and bondage a state of unspeakable joy, happiness and peace; and (4) the fourth Noble Truth declares the way that leads to nirvana. It is known as the Noble Eightfold Path, or sometimes referred to as the Middle Way, which consists of (1) right speech, (2) right action, (3) right livelihood, (4) right effort, (5) right mindfulness, (6) right concentration, (7) right views, and (8) right thought. The Eightfold Path, or the Middle Way, leads to insight and wisdom that dispel ignorance. The result is a state of perfect peace and bliss, which is nirvana. Nirvana, in the true sense of the term, is given by God in and through Jesus Christ, and not by human effort.

Thirdly, Islam, because of its Judeo Christian heritage has a certain degree of similarity, but it has its own distinctive features in terms of faith and practice, such as the literal understanding of the scriptures (the Koran) and the absolute monotheism of Allah. In this regard, a Christian approach to Islam in Asia must be positive. With understanding Christians should proclaim to the Islamic people of Asia the reliability of the gospel message as the Word of God, and the importance of God's revelation in the person of Jesus Christ as the Son of God. Any attempt to contextualize the gospel in an Islamic context should, therefore, begin with God and an emphasis on divine being, work, holy names, and the transcendent-immanent nature of God. A contextualized model of God will lead to an understanding of God in its fullness: as the rich deity of the Christian trinity who is revealed in Father, Son, and Holy Spirit. The doctrine of the Spirit has a special place in Islam, so it may lead to an understanding of Jesus Christ as the Son of God.

There are also attempts of contextualization of the gospel among the adherents of Confucianism, Shintoism, shamanism, and indigenous and primal religions. Wherever the gospel takes root, the people try to express their faith in Jesus Christ in the context of their language and culture, giving expression to indigenous forms of Christianity. So Christianity is not only something unique to European or Western way of life, it can be indigenous and contextual in Asia.

Although Christianity was born in Asia and only reached Europe later, the churches in Asia today (with the exception of Syrian Christians in South India) are products of the evangelical missionary awakenings of the European and North American churches. The Christianization was mainly done by missionaries from those countries, and they often collaborated with political powers in the colonial expansion, and enterprise. Thus, Christianity alienated itself from Asia's traditional and cultural heritage, and the Asian community way of life. Missionary Christianity was not truly Asian in faith or practice. Today, however, serious attempts are being made by Asian theologians in different Asian countries to make the gospel message relevant to each given context. Inculturation, indigenization, contextualization, and dialogue with the people of other faiths are being pursued in the Indian subcontinent with tangible results of success, and the fall-out effects are heard all over the world. Liberation theologies, such as *minjung* theology in Korea, *dalit* or tribal theology in India, feminist theology, and eco-theology are all echoes of new emerging trends in Asian theology today. All of these theological expressions are on the move in search of a relevant gospel message in order to give a contextual expression to the faith and practice of Christianity in each given situation or context in Asia. This is so done so that the gospel may become truly Asian.

The words of C.S. Song are appropriate as a conclusion to this essay:

> But we tend to forget that the theological truths we are after are with us all the time in Asia. There are signs of them in the marketplace. Their codes are written on the faces of women, men, and children in Asia. And symbols of theological truths hide themselves in the masses of Asian people. Where else then can we get glimpses of them if not in our cultures and histories? Life in Asia is theologically coded. To decode it we must immerse ourselves in it. Reappropriation and reexperience of that life with its cultural manifestations, religious beliefs, and historical hopes are essential parts of doing theology from the womb of Asia.[1]

Asian Christians need to reappropriate and reexperience the gospel in the context of our daily life, culture, and history. To use a phrase from C. S. Song again, "Ancient wisdom and faith," which may include the gospel and the faith of the church, "must be tested in the fire of the present life." The gospel and Christian faith must be tested in the fire of our daily life in Asia, to make it real to us and we may live by it. This is what the gospel means to us in Asia.

NOTES

[1]C. S. Song, *Theology from the Womb of Asia* (Maryknoll: Orbis, 1988), 18.

A Gospel of Covenant,
Community, and Kingdom

Eddie Kin-ming Ma

Before the treaty of Nanjing was signed in 1842, the first party of Christian missionaries came from Macau and landed on the Hong Kong Island looking for a suitable location to begin their work. In 1842, the first missionary to Hong Kong took up permanent residence; he was the Rev. Issachar J. Roberts, a Baptist, who arrived from Macau. A month later, he was joined by the Rev. J. Lewis Shuck and his wife, Henrietta. She was the first foreign woman to reside in Hong Kong.[1] A Baptist congregation was organized in Hong Kong in May 1842, and in July of the same year a chapel was opened on Queen's Road West.[2]

This small chapel became the first Baptist church in Hong Kong in 1901, and was called the Hong Kong Chinese Baptist Church. The church was organized as a self-supporting congregation with thirty-eight members. Later she became the grandmother and mother of all the Baptist churches in Hong Kong. Since early in this century Baptists have become the largest denomination in Hong Kong. Today there are more than 110 churches and chapels. Anglicans and Methodists arrived after Baptists to begin their work in Hong Kong. While Baptist strategies for missions focused on planting churches, Anglicans and Methodists sought to establish schools to educate the Chinese. The Morrison Education Society was formed to carry on this task. For many missionaries, educating was thought to the same thing as Christianizing. Carl Smith identifies such an approach as "educational imperialism," which merely reflects the basic western imperialistic approach of the nineteenth century.[3]

Several years ago, as Baptists celebrated the one hundred fifty year anniversary of the Baptists in Hong Kong, I discovered that we had made no effort to contextualize the gospel in Chinese soil. The form of Baptist life has been the same for one hundred fifty years. We have done very little work on contextualizing the gospel and the church; as a result, when crises arose, our Baptist brothers and sisters could not find any meaning of being Chinese, Baptist, and Christian. In this paper, I will first describe the context of Hong Kong, and then I will propose a model for the church that can express fully the incarnation of Jesus Christ in the Hong Kong context.

A Western City in Form,
but Chinese Tradition Oriented in Meaning

The result of modernization can be seen in Hong Kong, a 400 square mile colony. A recent survey shows that Hong Kong is the best place to do business in the world. Hong Kong is such a modern city that it compares well with other mega-cities in the world. Underneath this modern city, 99% of the residents are Chinese from the southern part of China. Hong Kong is a western city in form, but underneath it is a typical Chinese society. The traditional Chinese social order and the homologous cosmic order in which it is a part are basically Confucian in nature.[4] The Hong Kong Chinese worldview includes a mixture of Confucianism, Taoism, Buddhism, and Chinese folk religions. These perspectives become part of the culture that shape thought and action. In a Chinese mind, there is a mixture of "the doctrine of the mean" from Confucianism, the ideas that "weakness conquers strength," and "conformity to nature" from Taoism, and the Buddhist ideas of life, mercy, judgment and reincarnation. Besides these, there are also ideas of folk religion, notably attempts to manipulate the gods in order to bring prosperity.

A City in Crisis—the 1997 Issue as An Identity Crisis

The British government will end its sovereignty of Hong Kong in less than eight hundred days.[5] Hong Kong will once more become part of the People's Republic of China, as a special administrative zone. The imminent political and social change has brought the whole city to a point of crisis. Negotiations between Britain and China on the future of Hong Kong began in 1982. Since then, the Hong Kong people have struggled to arrive at ways to resolve the impending crisis. Some residents who have money or credentials have chosen to leave the colony to live in another country. Some residents take a permissive attitude, enjoying today, not thinking of tomorrow. Others are involved in politics, hoping to get the last chance of democracy before China takes over Hong Kong. Still others turn to religions, especially folk religion, because folk religion can offer easy answers to their problems.

The majority of the Hong Kong people do not believe the promise of the Chinese government to allow "one country two systems." The "one country" is China, that is, the People's Republic of China. The "two systems" have a double meaning, economic and political. In the economic sense, the "two systems" mean capitalism and socialism. In the political sense, the "two systems" refer to the centrally–controlled government structure and a "high degree of self-government" for Hong Kong.[6] The Hong Kong people are so close to China that they see the Chinese government promises one thing, only to do another thing. Many Hong Kong people have chosen to go somewhere else—a painful decision for them and their families. Those who cannot leave Hong Kong are forced to accept the reality that they will be under the reign of a communist government. Beneath the 1997 issue is the identity crisis. Hong Kong will be no longer a British colony, and many do not want to come under the rule of a communist government.

The Gospel as the Expression of Covenant People

The New Testament word *ecclesia* (church) has a much fuller meaning than the Chinese think of when they speak of "church" in their language.[7] The New Testament describes the church as a group of people who are called out by God to dedicate themselves in prayer and instruction. This group of people has a covenant with God through the blood of Jesus Christ. The Chinese people can understand the covenant concept because in the history of China, there have been established covenants with nearby nations for hundreds of years. In Confucian teaching, one needs to keep the covenant even to death.

The meaning of the church as a covenant people can help solve the identity crisis of the Hong Kong Chinese during this period of political transition. Our faith should not be built on the covenant made by the Sino-British governments. Our faith and identity should be built, instead, on the God who made and kept his covenant with Abraham, Isaac and Jacob. God will faithfully keep the covenant with us in the name of Jesus Christ, as long as we pledge allegiance to God. Through the visible local congregation to the world-wide covenant community, we can find our real identity in the truth of the Bible that will bring us through this crisis.

The Gospel as the Expression of Community People

Since 1982, people in Hong Kong began to emigrate to other countries. People remaining in Hong Kong suddenly lost most of the good friends they had had for years. Both adults and children experience the loss which leaves a vacuum in people's hearts. They need to rebuild their relationships. People need friends to support one another. The gospel of Jesus Christ reminds us that Christians are community people; we can experience the love of God through our brothers and sisters in the Lord. Because of Christ's love, we can build up a community with the same Lord and the same hope. Confucianism encourages the Chinese to take very seriously relationships; and this is also a key to unlock the Chinese worldview for Christian practice. Chinese culture stresses the values of duty, harmony and respect for authority. These are values that can fit into a new community of faith. The love of Christ will enrich our relationships. This community is called together to be in fellowship with God and with one another. This community is in the world but not of the world. Its ethics and values are over this world. This community is commissioned to go into the world.

The Gospel as the Expression of Kingdom People

The biblical truths of covenant and community also help us to understand that we are more than a group of people coming together for fellowship, we are identified as kingdom people. We are the agents of the kingdom of God. As agents of the kingdom, our responsibility is to be a community of witness and justice. In a period of political transition we need to uphold the value of justice that is revealed in the Bible. We do not need to be afraid to speak the truth, even if it means to stand against the government. Most importantly, the kingdom people will cling their hope on the kingdom of God. Hope in a new community will be the answer for most of the Hong Kong Chinese who are without any hope for the future.

Conclusion

This paper is an attempt to take seriously the context of expressing the nature of the gospel of Jesus Christ as found in the community of faith. The truth of *ecclesia* will help us to meet the needs of the Hong Kong Chinese when they experience the crisis of a political transition. The expression of the gospel as found among covenant people is a solution to the coming identity crisis. The expression of the gospel as community people is a solution to relational crisis. The expression of the gospel as a kingdom people is a solution to future crisis. My prayer is not only writing about contextualization but really putting it into practice in my own church, among my own people, in my own land, so that the Hong Kong Chinese may fully understand what the gospel means to them.

NOTES

[1]Carl T. Smith, *Chinese Christians: Elites, Middlemen, and the Church in Hong Kong* (Hong Kong: Oxford University Press, 1985), 2.

[2]Ibid., 3.

[3]Ibid., 32.

[4]Siu Kai Lau, *The Ethos of the Hong Kong Chinese* (Hong Kong: Chinese University Press, 1989), 4.

[5]This paper was presented on August 2, 1995.

[6]Peter K. H. Lee, "Contextual Theology: The Hong Kong 1997 Question as a Case Study," *Ching Feng* 37:3 (1994) 148–149.

[7]There are two terms to describe the church in Chinese language. *Laai baai tong* means the building of worship; *gaau wui* means teaching assembly.

Part Three
Accents from Southeast Asia

A Gospel of Reconciliation, Identity, and Purpose

Ken Manley

An understanding of what Christian obedience means has always been shaped by time and place. Our country is defined as the South by its very name, Australia (*terra australis*). We proudly accept that we are a people from "down under." Nonetheless, our name, given by the European North, is attached to a very ancient continent. It was there, and inhabited, long before any European explorer cast a possessive eye towards it.

Our continent is in an Asian and Pacific neighborhood. We are half a world away from the old orders and the tired voices of Europe. More recent European arrivals to this land have been slow to understand Australia in the way that the first residents did. Therefore, if we are to raise questions about the gospel in Australia, we first must ask, "Which Australia?" Do we mean the Australia of the white, middle class Anglo-Saxons? Do we mean the Australia of the Aborigines, who largely are dispossessed and marginalized? Or do we mean the Australia that includes a bewildering range of ethnic and cultural origins: European and Asian (115 national groups, one ethnic broadcaster covers 54 languages, 26% of contemporary Australians were born "overseas")?

What impact has the gospel had on these different Australias? Has the gospel played any role in fashioning a true sense of community in such a diverse society? Has the gospel become an integral part of Australian culture? The answers to these questions must be hesitant, because the gospel has played only a minor, if significant, role in the great south land. While we are genuinely grateful for faithful Christians who brought the gospel to these ancient shores, we also face urgent challenges in relating that gospel to the contemporary culture of Australia.

Australians characteristically suffer from a deep silence in the face of the mysteries of our continent and our life. We tend to dismiss what appears wordy and intellectual, preferring, instead the active approaches of a pragmatist. So, much of our religious experience has never been spoken. We did not think that there could be any theological interest in our story. But, as with the stories of all people, ours does invite theological reflection, especially when we see ourselves as a people "down under" in more than one sense.

Theologians are concerned to reflect on many themes, including those of defeat, isolation, failure, lostness, suffering and hope. These themes are the very essence of the Australian story. Remember the headlines of the story: The British arrived in 1788 to establish a gaol, (i.e., a prison colony), on the other side of the world from their "civilization." It was, to be sure, a barbaric concept that was cruelly executed. Recall, too, how those first arrivals dispossessed and oppressed the original residents of our land while they—the brutalized, exiled Europeans—sought a future in a strange place. Their new world was different and hostile, contributing factors in the construction of what could be called the first post-Christian society. Through the sorry events of all the bitterness there emerged a united people who came to take a place (to their own surprise!) on the stage of history, still cringing at their cultural inferiority.

Poets, novelists, dramatists and historians have tried to interpret the story of the European heritage of Australia, but theologians have contributed only in the last two decades. Attempts to create a so-called "gum leaf" theology, and to recreate God and Jesus in *ocker* (an Australian term that means "slang") terms have been failures. Much work towards contextualizing the gospel yet needs to be done.

Three affirmations that offer pointers to the theological issues needing further exploration in the Australian context include the role of the gospel in reconciliation, identity, and purpose.

Reconciliation

The gospel means reconciliation in a place of alienation. For the Aborigines, the coming of the gospel was accompanied by a white invasion. The Aborigines had been here for at least 40,000 years. God was already here, as in every part of creation. The first evangelicals came as military chaplains, a part of the "moral order," and failed to discern the spirituality of the "heathen," even if they were prepared to argue for compassion and justice. However falteringly, these evangelicals brought a knowledge of Christ.

Today white Australians have a national guilt about the past and also the present, because Aborigines truly are "down under" members of our society. Some Christians are in the forefront of supporting the granting of land rights to our original inhabitants, and in recognizing the depths of Aboriginal spirituality. There are, in fact, proportionally more Christians among Aboriginal people than among non-Aboriginal Australians. Baptists have led the way in some significant attempts to relate traditional Aboriginal culture and the Christian message. But the main theological challenge and the central mission imperative is to embody the reconciling power of the gospel in a divided society.

Identity

The gospel means identity in a place of exile. The theme of exile resonates with the Australian experience. The first European settlers were outcasts from Britain, separated from their families and any hope for respectability. Non convict settlers longed for "home," as Australians called Britain until a few decades ago. Cut off from all that was "beautiful" and "civilized," they hungered for a word of recognition. What the poet A. D. Hope saw as "monotonous tribes" surviving as "second-hand Europeans" living "timidly on the edge of alien shores" is true for Australian Christianity.

There is also a strong cultural trend for the exiled and isolated Australian to see himself, or herself as a battler: never quite able to get on top; always the underdog. The theme runs through our poems and stories. The outback battler, though in fact far removed from the urban dwellers who make up most of the population, remains a self-image that is important for Australians. Resentful of authority, devoted to knocking down the "tall poppy" (i.e., a significant achiever), the Australian rejects a church that has been aligned with civil and moral authority. The gospel of a weakness made perfect in suffering (cf. 2 Cor 12.1-10) should appeal to the Australian. We need a theology that insists we are not a rubbish people, but a graced people. We need a theology that gives hope to those on the margins of our society.

Purpose

The gospel means purpose in a place of emptiness. Our literature brims with descriptions of a spiritual vacuum. Novelist Patrick White identifies "the Great Australian Emptiness," and historian Manning Clark (the leading historian of our generation) calls Australia "the Kingdom of Nothingness." The vast Australian desert is now being appreciated as a place of silence that may yet offer meaning and, as was the case with another ancient desert, lead us to "the way of the Lord" (Isa 40).

The gospel, then, needs to be at the heart of an Australian theology that can address the themes of emptiness, spiritual hunger novelist Xavier Herbert has written of "the Great Australian Thirst" (that is "soul deep like the thirst of the damned in hell"), restlessness, search, and meaning. As R. Canning has observed this would be "a theology of the depths, exploring what is down under in people, continuously striving to find language to articulate the groaning of the Australian spirit."

Of course the gospel means much more in Australia, as it does elsewhere. Space forbids the exploration of other urgent themes: community in a place of multicultural diversity; transcendence in a secular and materialist society; acceptance and justice in a place of oppression; personhood and value in a technological world where economic rationalism holds sway; forgiveness and hope in a world of despair, especially for many women, the young (with an alarming number of teenage suicides), and the aged. A society facing complex ethical dilemmas and striving for moral values needs a church which models the Kingdom of God.

These questions remind us that while a local context is important, the universal and timeless message of the gospel draws us together in our quest for understanding our discipleship. It was an explorer from the North who imagined he had found the great south land who named it the "South Land of the Holy Spirit." We dare to hope and pray that this name for our land will become perfectly apt. God's Spirit was active here for millennia before Christ. But with the revelation of Christ we can now learn, Aboriginals and non-Aboriginals, even more of what it might mean to be the Great South Land of the Holy Spirit.

A Prayer for Indonesia

Billy Mathias

The gospel God gave to mankind through divine love for us is reflected in the words of Paul, "For whosoever shall call upon the name of the Lord shall be saved" (Rom 19.13), and the words recorded by Luke, "For with God nothing is impossible" (Luke 1.37). Through the power of God, new life in the kingdom of God comes to those who turn toward God (i.e., to those who are converted). God offers a simple gospel that human beings have made complicated by setting up barriers.

During the colonial days in Indonesia, the gospel was only for the Dutch settlers. As Dutch dominion grew, the gospel was shared among the Indonesian people, usually with the hope that Indonesian Christians would support the Dutch political system. In those days, becoming a Christian meant little more than gaining the rights that the Dutch enjoyed. Even now, since the days of independence, the gospel seems to be tied to the Dutch systems of society and culture. Christians build ethnic churches, so that Christians are divided among themselves by their own ethnic cultures and languages, while the larger society goes its way.

With the arrival of the new era of ethnic churches, and the touch of modern mission work, however, new churches are being formed, and are known as Indonesians churches. These new churches include more than one ethnic group. Missions began to grow in our land because there is no significant language barrier. The Bible can be printed in our national language and, therefore, is easily distributed throughout the twenty-seven provinces of Indonesia.

Despite the barriers of privilege and ethnic pride forged with human hands, through the simple gospel message many people in Indonesia are won to Christ. For example, after forty-three years, the

Baptist church, which had only four national members in 1952, had develop into 686 churches and missions by 1995. Baptist churches in Indonesia now have their own Union, and have launched a new program: "Developing in Independence to reach 2000–2." The "2000–2" means that by the year 2000 all Baptist churches that participate in The Indonesian Baptist Union, hope to have developed in their spiritual quality so that through their commitment, our congregations can double in size.

As we try to reach more people to Christ, another barrier has to be faced by Indonesian Christians. This barrier comes from within the church. Because most of our leaders studied in Europe or the United States, they came to Indonesia with various theological issues, that are not relevant to the spiritual needs of the Indonesian people. The co-operative culture—which is the lifestyle of the Indonesian people—is threatened by the individualistic lifestyle that prevails in the West. The western style of worship is still dominant in most churches, with the result that the gospel remains foreign to most people in Indonesia.

Because there are so many unreached people in Indonesia, some churches came to the conclusion that using a contextual approach to missions would be productive. For example, in my home province of West Java there is one large ethnic group called the Sudanese people. There are about 32 million Sudanese people. After 155 years of work among the Sudanese people only a few of them responded to the gospel. Through a contextual approach to reach the Sudanese, the Indonesian Bible Society printed the Bible in the Sudanese language. The style of worship using western musical instruments also is changing by using local musical instruments, which are well known to the people. Sitting during worship in expensive pews also must be changed to the custom of sitting on a mat or the floor. Such simple changes can make the gospel more available to the Sudanese.

What we need is the simple biblical gospel that focuses on God's love for every person on earth. We do not need theological issues that can divide the churches and stop our mission to unreached people. We need to live according to the teaching of the gospel, and we need cooperative prayers to God that we may live the gospel that we preach.

Pray for us in Indonesia as we try to reach the 2000–2 goal. Also pray for our witness among the Sudanese people as we strive to live the simple gospel.

A Gospel Not Too Foreign, Yet Not Foreign Enough

Brian Smith

If New Zealand is part of anything geographically, it is part of Southeast Asia. As far as its culture is concerned, however, New Zealand is western. Migration beginning in the nineteenth century and since continuing, particularly from Britain, means that a large proportion of New Zealanders are European in origin. Today Europeans account for 80% of the population. Indigenous Maori make up a further 10%, while immigrant groups who have come from the various Pacific Islands since the 1960s total 4%.

If we are to address the question of the contextualization of the gospel in New Zealand, it is clear that any detailed answer would have to include Maori and Pacific Island expressions of the faith. Only the majority culture will be dealt with in this paper, however. In relation to the dominant culture the answer to the question, "Has the gospel been contextualized in New Zealand?" must be, "Yes." Insofar as the gospel has been at home in Europe for over 1000 years, it is this faith that has been transplanted to New Zealand. Having said this however, the most marked feature of New Zealand's recent religious history is the disappearance from society of the penumbra of Christian nominalism. This feature is well symbolized by comparing the Billy Graham evangelistic campaigns in 1959 and 1995. In 1959, Billy Graham held a series of hugely successful "crusades" throughout the country. Preaching "the Bible says," Graham presented a traditional gospel message that found wide acceptance by virtue of a residual Christian understanding in the population at large. In mid-century, many New Zealanders still had some idea of what it was to be a "sinner," to be "lost," to need to "decide for Christ" and return to the fold of the church. In March of 1995, however, when Graham made his world-wide appeal by satellite, that former residual Christian understanding had disappeared. The evangelist had no underlying ethos to tap, no half-remembered Sunday School stories, no sense of the Bible as "the Word of God," and no expectation that the name "Christ" is anything more than an expletive. Over the last generation in New Zealand the movement of modern western society has effectively pushed the gospel to the margin of consciousness and society. From being part of the general fabric of people's understanding, as recently as 1959, the gospel has become an eccentric viewpoint at the edge of society in 1995.

Gospel Relevance

Faced with a situation where the gospel is marginalized, the urgent questions for the churches have been, "How do we contextualize the gospel?" and "How do we make it relevant in a post-Christian society?" The answers have been almost unanimous. First we must identify the modern questions that need to be addressed. Then we must translate the gospel answers into currently understandable conceptualities. An example is a cartoon that ran in an ecclesiastical paper. Imagine in the upper left a church building floating on a cloud. On the ground is the mass of humanity carrying banners with slogans, including, "Housing is a Right," "Welfare Cuts Bleed," "Health and Justice and Work for All." On the right is a small group that has managed to get some ropes around the church building. They are straining with all their might to get it off its cloud and down to earth where the real action is. Christians who are concerned to be relevant say that unless the church addresses the real needs of people, the Christian message will continue to fall on deaf ears.

In line with such a glimpse of the church, the churches in New Zealand have made a serious effort to address the social and political concerns of the day. In an increasingly dysfunctional society, the helping acts of the church have proliferated endlessly. But while people have been glad for our good works (often carried out with enormous government subsidies), they have stayed away from having anything to do with the gospel. Church attendance has dropped in inverse proportion to the number of good works. Today, on any given Sunday, only ten percent of the population of New Zealand can be found in a church of any kind. In the interests of accessibility, the gospel has been translated, but the end result has been a reductionism that has transformed the gospel message into the truisms of its hearers. For good cause the church is widely regarded as simply another group in society that is concerned with doing good.

An Attractive Community

The reason for the failure of a well-intentioned attempt at a contextualization of the gospel is clear. From the church side, the problem has been the irrelevance of the gospel. From the point of view of society, however, the issue is the irrelevance of the gospel. Or to put it another way, where the church has seen the gospel as "foreign" and needing to be translated, New Zealand society sees the gospel as not "foreign" enough to even be interesting.

The task facing the church therefore, is not contextualization, but its reverse—the creation of a counter-culture that has an attractive power. What is needed is not a church that affirms society's fundamental beliefs, but a church that challenges those assumptions, a church that, for instance, denies the all-pervasive individualism of western society and its conviction that the good life consists in consumption.

If the church is to be counter-culture, it is important to say that the life of the congregation must be attractive. In typical fashion, western Christianity has shifted responsibility for an attractive lifestyle from the congregation to the individual believer. Thus, in theory, each Christian is a virtuoso practitioner of the faith, whose performance is supposed to elicit admiration, and the question "Why?" from workmates, relatives, and friends. All too often, however, our individual performance is judged sub-standard. Non-Christian observers expect perfection, and are inclined to be severe judges of our efforts to be followers of Jesus. However the point of our being followers of Jesus is not that we turn in star performances as individuals, but that we are members of a community that lives differently. Only by holding hands and living as disciplined congregations do we have any chance of offering an attractive alternative to the prevailing culture.

And when we speak to others, it will not be so much about my experience of happiness and a sense of peace, but about our experience of living together in a new kind of way. In contrast to the subjective nature of the former (so-called New Agers claim similar things), the life of a community in which people love one another is objective and visible. It is the existence of this new kind of community that witnesses to the power of the gospel. To quote Leslie Newbigin:

> How is it possible that the gospel should be credible, that people should come to believe that the power which has the last word in human affairs is represented by a man hanging on a cross? I am suggesting that the only answer, the only hermeneutic of the gospel is a congregation of men and women who believe it and live by it.[1]

NOTES

[1]Lesslie Newbigin. *The Gospel in a Pluralist Society* (London: SPCK, 1989), 227.

Part Four
Accents from Latin America

A Gospel of Hope

Rolando Gutiérrez-Cortés

As Baptists in Mexico, we can say that the gospel of God in Jesus
Christ means salvation to be shared in a society that is made up of
fifty-six ethnic groups with 225 languages. Sharing the gospel must
include evangelism, church planting and church development.

In the exercise of a permanent Christian education program, we
foster in our local churches the notion of the priesthood of all believers. In trying to encourage communications under the principle of
freedom of conscience, we respect the precept of not speaking on
behalf of either all Christians, or of all Baptists of our area.

We applaud this encounter. We have a theological education
program for the whole country which includes seminaries, Bible insti-
tutes, theological schools, theological education programs by exten-
sion, and oral education centers, all which encourage the articulation
of our faith. Where we have been called upon to say we are doing in
Mexico, we are glad to say that everything we do in our regions is for
the enlightenment of our historical expression as a Baptist World Alliance.

In Mexico, we have a Board of World Missions. We have been
cooperating with Baptists in Spain and Honduras; and we also have a
Board of National Missions, which is going forward with a self development commitment in thirty–two out of fifty–six ethnic groups.

To share what the gospel means to us demands a delimitation of
the influences we have received, and will continue to receive. We
must also note the influences we have exercised and continue to exercise. Thus, to share in this workshop designed to explore the meaning
of the gospel is a privilege because it means not only sharing, but
nourishing ourselves.

Baptist work in Mexico officially began with the organization of the First Baptist Church in Monterrey, Nuevo León, January 30, 1864. The National Baptist Convention was organized in September, 1903 only two years before the organization of Baptist World Alliance in London, 1905. Mexican Baptists were represented in London by Dr. Alejandro Treviño, and have the privilege of being founding members of the Alliance. As in all areas of the world, the balanced growth of our churches has depended upon the support on the articulation of faith in which we have been able to develop permanently.

Baptist theological education in Mexico, along with the social action it encouraged, focuses on strengthening our work. There are thirty-four theological schools in thirty-eight regional conventions which form our national convention. There are twelve institutions recognized by the Theological Education Program of our convention in different regions of the country. They are Baptist Theological Institute, Chihauhua, Chihuahua; Baptist Theological Seminary of La Laguna, Torreón, Coahuila; Emmanuel Baptist Theological Seminary, Guadalajara, Jalisco; "Cosme G. Montemayor" Theological Institute, Matamoros, Tamaulipas; "God with Us" Baptist Theological Seminary, Mexicali, Baja California Norte; Baptist Theological Seminary of Veracruz, Coatzacoalcos, Veracruz; Baptist Theological Seminary, San Jeronimito, Guerrero; Baptist Theological Seminary of the Border, Ciudad Juárez, Chihuahua; Baptist Theological Seminary of Mérida, Yucatán; and Baptist Theological Seminary of Sonora, Sonora.

There also are two supporting institutions at the national level. The "Dr. G. H. Lacy" Baptist Theological Seminary is in Oaxaca, in an Indian region in the South of Mexico, and the Mexican Baptist Theological Seminary is in Mexico, D.F., working at bachelor's and master's degree levels, with the support of a staff of foreign teachers who have come here to help.

Twenty-two additional theological institutions look after the specific needs of their areas and respond to their environment with their own resources.

To consider research, teaching and transmission of information as the tripod of the academic task, permits us to evaluate the role developed in each case.

Baptist presence in thirty–two out of the fifty–six ethnic groups of the country demands coordination and contextualization in theological expression. This is the reason for a Theological Education Program at a national level that tries to coordinate the evangelistic and missionary interests of the Baptist Convention of Mexico, and encouraging our denominational identity through the constant feedback of our beliefs, principles and articles of faith.

In thinking to place ideas in order, history has witnessed that we publicly have made known that our Baptist beliefs shape our missionary mentality. In reflecting to restructure our thinking, it has been to witness that Baptist principles support our actions as the lives of our predecessors faithfully prove that the Bible was their rule of faith and behavior.

Alien to dogmatism and with the Bible as the rule of faith, our confessions of faith have been considered to help articulate and systematize beliefs and principles which support our theological, ecclesiastical and missionary work and, at the same time, have enabled us to serve and speak with others in an open dialogue that nourishes and multiplies our testimony.

As a historical observation regarding Latin America in general, my impression from Mexico is that there have been theological and institutional approaches at the inter-denominational levels; but that at the denominational level, there has been a closer approach of leaders than of theologians and institutions.

The peculiar historical expression of the gospel in Mexico (and elsewhere in Latin America) has been evangelism and Christian education with "only Christ saves" as the central theme. Recently, there also has been a growth in missionary stewardship and service with an emphasis on a theology of hope, which highlights the articulation of faith achieved by the gospel in our culture. Much of the missionary success in Mexico is due to theological education in all of its formal and informal manifestations. Influences of hopeful theology have been felt interactively through forums such as the Latin American Fraternity of Theology, and through the participation of Fraternities of Theological Schools. These groups have strengthened and fostered the development of a distinct understanding of the gospel in our area of the world.

An important by-product of the missionary stewardship found in Mexico, and other Latin American countries, is an impact on broader culture and society. For example, the emphasis on Christian education has enriched fundamental teaching in all levels of education, from elementary schools through the universities. Related is the growing interest in literacy and community developments, since the churches are involved in the basic educational needs of their communities. Also, the impact of missionary stewardship has been felt in the areas of health care and health education.

While the work of contextualizing the gospel in Mexico is succeeding in the areas noted above, there are still frontiers to be explored. Communication and technologies are waiting for gospel influences. We need to turn our attention to the arts, for example, especially theater, television, and radio. The field of journalism is also fertile for the gospel.

Our testimony can be improved daily. The twentieth century clearly marks progress of our corporate service in the world as Baptist World Alliance. Justice and peace in a conscious cultivation of freedom of conscience, have been significant aspects of the gospel among the people of Mexico, and the rest of the world. It is a service that has been appreciated through our work as Baptists. This is the reason why the years from 1905 to 1995 have been a fruitful road traveled by churches, conventions, service institutions, and particularly, our schools where the theological tasks are pursued.

A Gospel Lived

Guillermo I. Catalán

Is the culture of a particular country a friend or an enemy to the gospel? The answer to this fundamental question will reveal the philosophy of ministry of those who are leaders among the people of God. Most certainly the answer will reveal an essential factor in the concept of the nature and mission of the church in a given culture. A helpful and authentic answer to the question of culture's impact on the gospel requires an integral concept of humanity, an integral concept of the gospel, and an integral concept of salvation.

Chile, like other Latin American countries, received contact with the gospel first through Catholicism (since 1500) and later through evangelical influences and activities which began a century ago. From the Catholic perspective, evangelization came to Chile with the Spanish conquerors, who from the time of the conquest and the period of colonization were responsible for bringing to the country a " gospel" that already had suffered under the process of sixteen centuries of development in Europe. The Christianization of Latin American culture emanated from an ecclesiastic apparatus (the institutionalized Roman Church) that wielded a strong authority (including religious, moral and social-political). The all pervasive influence incorporated the magic-religious elements of the native Latin American culture, and used them in the "evangelizing education" that the church sought to develop, trying thereby to exercise a meaningful influence in the society and in the culture. The result of this history has been a religious expression in Latin America which is an amalgamation of pagan elements alongside those faith elements of Christianity producing a syncretism.

From the evangelical perspective, on the other hand, the evangelization of the country began with the arrival of evangelical colonists, and also the arrival of Anglo-Saxon and other European missionaries who, upon entering Latin American culture, challenged it with an ethnocentric tonality. Through their missionaries, the gospel came and remained clothed in the spirit and wrappings of the culture from which it proceeded. To some extent the cultures of the European missionaries have been superimposed on the Latin American cultural background. Examples of such an influence are the music and instruments that are used in worship services, and the buildings of the principal Baptist churches in important cities of our countries. These, we recognize without minimizing their values, have limited options and alternatives from the native culture.

The Chilean Context

When we have to refer to the "adequate articulation" of the gospel, we must say that it cannot be defined as adequate, because our culture does not reflect the influences of an authentic gospel. By way of illustration, some statistics that have been released by the National Institute of Statistics in Chile provide a glimpse of contemporary Chile.

> In Chile there are nearly five million children, all of whom are subjects of "legal rights" according to national laws and international agreements. Nevertheless, this reality that exists on paper, requires profound cultural changes that avoid, for example, that in the country more than 50% of those children live in conditions of extreme poverty or that maintain an extremely high index of child abuse[1]

> Information released by the UNICEF and the Corporation of Child Abuse (statistics from 1989 to 1990) reveals to us that Chile is the third country in the world, after Japan and Germany, in relation to maltreatment of children. This information says that 63% of the children are victims of physical violence, and of these 34% suffer permanent after-effects, 14.5% of the children have suffered psychological violence, 11% of this number is found in low social strata, and that 24.6% is found in high social strata.[2]

The following numbers have been published with regard to abortion: "35% of pregnancies in Chile are terminated by induced abortion, with an average of 480 abortions daily."[3] The National Women's Service, in a recent report, indicated "that one out of every four women in Chile is victim of some type of violence; 33.5% suffer psychological violence and 26.2% suffer physical abuse and violence."[4]

The National Institute of Statistics, in its final report of the National Census of the Population taken in 1992, indicates "that of 4,899,720 married persons, 537,444 are not living together, 324,926 are formally separated, and 30,656 have annulled their marriage."[5] That is to say that 18.3% of Chilean marriages have failed. Nevertheless, Chile is one of the three countries of the world that does not accept divorce (the other two are Ireland and the Vatican).

What has been sketched above are some very real examples of the true situation in Chile that show clear evidence that the articulation of the gospel has not been adequate in our culture. CELAM III (the Council of Latin American Bishops), in Puebla, Mexico in 1979, recognized the necessity of a new evangelization for Latin America. Until now the "new evangelization" has been, as it were, the taking out of memory trunks old Catholic traditions that no longer have a significant impact on the lives of Chile's people.

From the evangelical point of view however, we can not say much either. First, because there has not been much interest among evangelicals (including Baptists) in social problems or, made interest in recovering part of the larger community in a more significant way (although in these last years this aspect has been improved upon). And second, because it is understood that the proclamation of the gospel has to do with the "salvation of souls" and so our main task is preeminently spiritual.

Lamentably, much of our evangelical leadership does not have an adequate theology of the culture (recall our initial question) and when I mentioned that the gospel which came from an evangelical tradition remained wrapped in the clothing and spirit of that culture, I was referring to the fact that our "evangelists" considered that their own culture came to our culture with the gospel and in this way imposed a style of dressing, types of architecture, music styles and a series of things related to the spread of the gospel in our land. Who would not wish that our cultures were Christianized to become the pure lifestyle that biblical principles can produce, such as was with the European and

North American culture? Chile, and the rest of Latin American, continues to be a missionary project, until the articulation of the gospel is adequate for and in our culture.

According to the last census, the evangelical presence in Chile is about 20% of the population, while Catholic sources indicate that only 12% of Chilean Catholics are active in the life of the church. From the perspective of available opportunities, the truth is that evangelicals have great difficulty in taking advantage of the open doors before us. We are a minority but we are an important minority. Everyone, everywhere in Chile, has a good concept of evangelical Christians, especially because of their reputation for good citizenship. Likewise, the evangelical devotion and worship is recognized as being simple, sincere and direct, fostering in the rest of society a religious and spiritual conscience.

From this view point, the gospel, in spite of the limitations of its presentation, has made an impact, especially in the field of ethics and morality. But there are many other areas that are still virgin as regards the impact of the gospel. The political arena, economics, arts, sciences, and sports, for example, are open to the influence of the gospel. A Christian athlete may be called *El Bíblico* (the biblical one) while a Christian workman or day-laborer may be called *El Hermano* (brother). It may be that these terms are sometimes used in an offensive way, or it may be that the person is being recognized because he practices his beliefs, but even this is the testimony of the impact of the gospel on the culture. Even so, our culture continues to be a missionary project, a missionary field.

One of my colleagues in Santiago shared the following experience. A member of my Sunday School class noticed that a group of evangelical workmen in a certain factory began to get together at lunch break to pray. Each time the group was bigger. The activity reached the ears of the owner of the shop. He said that in his business he would not accept proselytism, even less from *canutos* (a deriding term for evangelical Christians). He said that he would fire them all, but before doing so he wished to talk with them and to inform them personally of his decision. He named a day and hour to meet with them. The evangelical laborers gathered, fearful because they were going to lose their jobs. When the owner of the business came to the meeting he looked at the men for a long time, but he could not speak.

He was mute for a while. When he recovered his voice, he said: "I am standing before the best people of my business, my very best workmen. You are my best people. I was mistaken. Excuse me."

Even though it is still difficult for Chilean evangelicals to use the different means of communication such as press, radio or television, still the gospel has penetrated in our society through the people of God. The communicators are the neighbors, families, colleagues in the work place, students in all educational levels who have taken upon themselves the responsibility of transmitting this Christ-centered gospel, a peculiarity of the evangelical message, which has as its only source of authority the Scriptures and which is translated into an ethic of faith in daily life.

This gospel continues to satisfy the need that people have for God, the need to be someone, the need for hope, the need to be able to administer wisely the context in which we live, the need to love and to be loved. The great need of society that pressed on the people of God is for a theology of the culture that is product of an integral concept of humanity, an integral concept of the gospel, an integral concept of salvation.

Words from the New Testament book of John hear witness to the land of gospel we need:

> And the Word, that was God, became flesh and dwelt among men full of grace and truth. And that same Word prayed saying: "Father, as you sent me in to the world, so I have sent them into the world. Now they are not of the world but they are in the world. I pray not that you would take them out of the world but that you will keep them from evil."

NOTES

[1]Claudia Villalobos. *Diario La Epoca*, 6 de Junio de 1995.
[2]María P. López H. *Diario El Mercurio*, 6 de Junio de 1995.
[3]Claudio Betsalel. *Revista Ercilla*, 5 de Agosto de 1994.
[4]S. Larraín. *Estudios De Prevalencia De La Violencia Intrafamiliar Y La Condiciion De La Mujer En Chile*. Informe Preliminar. Isis Internacional.
[5]*I.N.E. Informe Final Del Censo A La Poblacion De Chile*. 1992.

A Gospel Toward Maturity

Carlos Villanueva*

The theme of this workshop is, "What the gospel means to us." When we speak of "us," we refer to our specific situations, so I will begin by presenting our cultural roots.

When we speak of "culture,"[1] we refer to the "conjunction of data—information—which every person receives from the human environment in which he or she is inevitably inserted, and by which he or she is also conditioned."[2] The "information" may include language, productive structures, educational methods, as well as other shaping factors.

Human beings are born and develop responding to two types of information that they receive passively. The first is constituted by genetic information, which varies from individual to individual and which, in certain measure, sets boundaries within which they respond to their cultural environment. The second is formed by the information which an individual receives from their social environment from birth (or even conception), which may be called culture. It is this latter source which, given concrete stimuli, intends to elicit certain responses from the individual. Therefore, if one should seek that which conditions behavior, such conditioning is not determined either solely by genetic information or solely by cultural information, but rather through a combining of both. One should specify that both types of information together produce yet another type of information, a second order of data. This second order has to do with the manner in which first order data is received and appropriated by the individual.

Lastly, it is necessary to mention that "culture" is a conjunction of functionally reciprocal elements: the specific type of language

*Translated by Bob Adams.

which is united with an internal form of organizing time and space, is in turn related to the transmission of culture (i.e., education), which in turn is related to the organization of family and community life. The conjunction of reciprocally organized and functioning elements in humanity may be called "structure."

The foregoing introduction should lead us to think that this accumulation of received information (what we mean by "culture") has conditioned us toward an interpretation of the gospel in this part of the world.

Factors in the Formation of Our Culture

We begin by mentioning that the message of the gospel arrived in our continent from Spain by means of "evangelization." The *encomienda* was an institution by means of which the Spanish crown aspired to carry out the primordial end of its conquest: the evangelization of the gentile races.

José Garcia Hamilton, in his book, *Los orígenes de nuestra cultura autoritaria* (*The Origins of Our Authoritarian Culture*) applies to our context the thesis of Max Weber.[3] In his work, García Hamilton affirms that although "there are differences among the Latin American countries, most of the elements herein described are common property, which means that one may speak of an hispanoamerican culture which is authoritarian and backward economically."[4]

This "evangelization" of Latin America helped create an authoritarian and divided society: Christians and infidels, aristocracy and common people, military and civil, clergy and laity.

Factors in the Formation of Our "Evangelical Culture"

García Hamilton's thesis is very attractive: we accuse Catholicism of all the difficulties we face. Even though it is true that part of our "Latin American problem" has its origin in that particular interpretation of what the gospel is which we received through the colonialists, we should ask ourselves what we evangelicals have done, as we attempt to support our culture.

We should begin by recognizing that Protestant Christianity arrived in Latin America already as an "imported product" from the hands of immigrants[5] such as missionaries who came from the "northern" powers.[6] Thus from the beginning, it was necessary to deal with a form of religion foreign to national values.

From that beginning era, one may note certain characteristics. We should remember that the "transplanted churches" were important to the immigrants in that they helped maintain ethnicity, in which the language and old customs were preserved. It was not until a later time that those ethnic churches began any work in relation to the society which surrounded them. It should be remembered that Pablo Besson—the founding Baptist in Argentina—came to Argentina as a pastor of an ethnic church in Santa Fe.

At the same time there were negative results: alongside the faith, there was a tendency to import a particular ideology, an interpretation of reality, that had not emerged in our land. Also a kind of subculture was created. The immigrants did not involve themselves in the social environment in which they lived. The church was a refuge in which they isolated themselves, because they had a negative opinion of our Latin American culture. As Tito Paredes notes:

> There are persons, peoples or nations that think and believe that their language, their lifestyle, their customs, their form of thinking and acting are better or superior to those of other persons, peoples or nations.[7]

Such was the situation of the founders of evangelical and Baptist life in Argentina, and the rest of Latin America.

It wasn't until the most recent times that it has been valid to say, "We are entering a new situation for the church in Latin America. We are not only in a third or fourth generation of evangelicals, but we are already recognized as...a reality that is part of that which is normal."[8] Or, as A. Rembao qualifies, Hispanic protestantism succeeded to cultural autonomy.[9]

If the 1930–1960 years can be denominated, a time of development not only in numbers but also in our insertion in society, the 1980s represent a time of an even greater growth. This growth took place out of what has been called, "popular protestantism."[10] The impact of pentecostal "growth" has moved many of our churches to adopt this type of protestantism. In some sense, this represents a regression from the insertion of the gospel in society.[11]

In spite of this apparent cultural autonomy on the part of our churches, the negative results of the arrival of the gospel to our cultural situation continue—ideologizing and self-marginization.

Implications for Latin America

We are no longer able to blame either our Catholic cultural context, or those things which our evangelical pioneers did for the Christian situation today. We are faced with the challenge of evaluating our own attitudes and, from there, we are faced with the challenge to press on toward maturity.

We have not outgrown the authoritarianism which we inherited from Catholicism, which gave rise to an extreme *caudillismo* (dictatorship on some level). We must remember that democratic ideals were not applied in the past. We have before us the danger of authoritarianism in our churches, which were, before, models of participatory democracy.

We have not been able to have much influence in our cultural context, in proportion to our growth. In some sense, we are once more in danger of isolating ourselves from the reality which surrounds us. Evangelical participation in the larger community life has not increased in spite of some isolated examples. On the contrary, the evolution of evangelicals—or should we say devolution—of late has carried us backward toward to a faith that concentrates on the personal and individual as opposed to the social.

The prophetic voice of the church is not heard in our community. The reality of our society is one in which contrasts are more marked, homelessness increases, extreme poverty grows, and the marginalized are pushed further out. The challenge lies in fighting against all these and other forms of discrimination.

On the other hand, and even with all the limitations which we have described, the message of the gospel gave light to many inhabitants of our lands, helped them to recognize themselves as important, dignified them as persons.

In summary, we Baptists in Latin America are still fighting against social currents that prevent our full participation in society at the same time that we are challenging ourselves to a more ample involvement in the community in order to bring the complete gospel to the whole of society.

NOTES

[1]E. Chiavacci, "Cultura," *Diccionario Teológico Interdisciplinar* (Salamanca, Sígueme, 1982), II, 230.

[2]Tito Paredes, "Evangelio y Culture," CLADE III (FTLA), 136–137, speaks of "two foci" of "culture," one [focus] traditional in the sense of formation, and another wide-ranging and inclusive. It is to this second focus which signifies "culture" that I refer.

[3]Max Weber, *La Etica Protestante y el Espíritu del Capitalismo*. J. I. García Hamilton summarizes Weber's thesis noting that in the European countries which were "mixed" religiously, owners and managers of businesses were, generally, Protestants. This preeminence over Catholics in economic activities was true not only in nations or zones where Protestants were politically minorities. Majority or minority, Protestants forged ahead in productive activities. Weber looked for the answer to this phenomenon in ideals. In the case of Catholics—the monk, the "spiritual" over the "material." In the case of Luther, each Christian should accept his "secular" task as a sacred mission. García Hamilton summarizes, "Until Luther, a 'saint' was one who left the world and became a monk, joining a monastery. From the German reformer on, a 'saint' was one who abandoned the monastery and honorably worked the soil" (158).

[4]José García Hamilton, *Los orígenes de nuestra cultura autoritaria*, 211.

[5]Pablo A. Deiros wrote, in his *Historia del Cristianismo en América Latina* (FTLA), 619, "The presence of Protestant colonials, with their families and religious traditions, made necessary a greater tolerance."

[6]From England, Anglican missionaries and pastors, from Europe, Pablo Besson, and from the United States.

[7]T. Paredes, quoted en F. Quicaña, *Evangelio y Cultura*, CLADE III (FTLA), 145.

[8]Emilio Castro, "La obra pastoral en el *kairos* latinoamericano," *Pastores del Pueblo de Dios en América Latina*, 12.

[9]A. Rembao, *Discurso a la Nación Evangélica* (Buenos Aires, Argentina: La Aurora), 87.

[10]P. Deiros and C. Mraida, *Latinoamerica en llamas* (Miami, Caribe, 1994), 114. Popular Protestantism expresses itself in the religious forms of classical pentecostalism, but with a strong emphasis on the emotional element and in the immediate perception of religious experience. It is almost always characterized by dependence on some charismatic leader and authoritarianism.

[11]On the other hand, one might conclude that it represents a contextualization into our cultural values.

Conclusion

Contemporary Gospel Accents:
What We Have Heard

Daniel Carro and Richard F. Wilson

What we have heard is clear: there is only one gospel of Jesus Christ. We have heard that confession, however, through diverse accents. The accents tell us as much about where the gospel is confessed as it does how the gospel is confessed in Africa, Asia, Southeast Asia, and Latin America. By listening to diverse accents we have been reminded that the gospel is both divine and human in its content and context. The diverse accents through which we have heard the gospel in the preceding pages reminds us that in its essence the gospel is transcendent even when it becomes immanent in finite cultures. The reminders are valuable because they call us back to the center of gospel which is the person and work of Jesus Christ, and they also spur us forward toward "the ends of the earth," regardless of where we identify the beginning of the earth.[1]

The essence of the gospel is like the essence of music. Music is music. Music is a unified form. Nevertheless, every culture and every composer underscores particular aspects of the rich elements that are encompassed by the one reality of music. African music, for example, emphasizes rhythm, while Latin music emphasizes melody, and Anglo-Saxon music explores harmony.

A similar thing happens with the essence of the gospel. Each culture interprets the gospel in particular ways, highlighting aspects of the one gospel that have peculiar meaning in a given context. Every culture sees the gospel of Jesus Christ from a unique point of view, and every individual participant of given culture interprets the gospel according to his or her more narrow perspectives within a culture.

Elevating a single interpretation of the gospel to the status of an absolute impoverishes the one gospel of Jesus Christ by denying the breadth and depth of the gospel as met in diverse cultural contexts. In contrast, when many perspectives of the gospel are seen together and heard through rich accents, the result is an enrichment of an understanding of the one gospel. What we have heard is an enriching intersection of confessions that have added to our understanding of the gospel. This was very clear in the addresses of this conference. Taken singularly and together, the presentations of the gospel stressed different accents of the gospel, according to the particular cultural setting in which each one of them live and toil.

At the same time there emerged some common themes of gospel interpretation that help us understand what an accent from the South—south of the equator, that is—sounds like. All of the participants hail from the so-called Third World, which the conference organizers preferred to call, geopolitically speaking, "the South." What we have heard includes the common themes spoken in a southern accent and the uncommon themes spoken in African, Asian, Southeast Asian, and Latin American cadences.

COMMON THEMES

Building upon Stephan B. Bevans's helpful *Models of Contextual Theology*,[2] we have heard clearly two common themes. We have heard of the significant impact missionaries from Europe and North American have had on the shape of gospel interpretations in the South. As the gospel has taken root in diverse soils we also have heard significant unrest about the captivity of gospel interpretations by European and North American cultures.

Missionary Impact on Gospel Accents

Beneath every spoken and written word in the heart of this book there is a two-pronged acknowledgement of the impact missionary activity has had in Africa, Asia, Southeast Asia, and Latin America. With sincere gratitude, all the accents we have heard report how the gospel came to them from the West and the North. The gratitude, however, is framed by the recognition that the missionaries also brought with them their cultures from the North and West, and that the missionaries seemed as intent on preaching their culture as they were committed to preaching the gospel.

The blending of the content of the gospel and its cultural wrapping is a danger of a "translational model" described by Bevans.[3] During the first waves of missionary activity, following a translation model is understandable as a naive approach to a complex task. Missionaries preached the gospel in ways appropriate to their home cultures. Styles of dress, musical forms, architectural plans, and institutional structures uncritically mimicked the looks and sounds of Christian groups in the North and the West. Thinking that the gospel was primarily a language event that merely could be translated into another language, the first missionaries were unaware that they had become evangelists of a culture as well as the gospel.

The theologians who spoke at our conference and whose presentations are included in this book are grateful that they heard Christ preached, but they have grown wary of the cultural forms of Christianity that accompanied the gospel and persist in the contemporary world. Their wariness raises legitimate and serious questions about the possibility of simply translating the gospel for other cultures. And their wariness drives them to find ways to preserve the integrity of the gospel while separating it from a foreign cultural garb.

Speaking in Native Languages

Responses to translation models of contextual theology appear to move toward two other models: a synthetic model, and a praxis model.[4] O. M. Rao brings the most pronounced accent of a synthetic model for contextual theology.[5] Writing with deep passion as a Christian and as a patriot of India, Rao lists many of the excesses of missionaries who preached a "captive gospel" (captive to their home culture) as a backdrop for equally passionate appeals for Christians in India to live as Indians for Christ. Beginning with concerns about the integrity of Indian Christians's appreciation for their struggle for independence from Britain, and ranging through appeals for Indian Christians to allow the gospel to become incarnate within the rich culture of India, Rao works as a weaver intent on pulling together the heart of the gospel for the heart of India.

Osadolor Imasogie also shows an inclination toward a synthetic model of contextual theology, with a decided pastoral bent.[5] His great concern for the gospel in Nigeria is that when many Nigerians face spiritual crises they revert to traditional religious practices. The reason for Nigerian Christians seeking traditional African religious solutions to contemporary crises, Imasogie laments, is that the gospel has not been proclaimed in ways that are relevant to African culture. There is a deep appreciation and reverence for the spirit world among Africans, yet the gospel, despite its explicit attention to demons and spiritual powers of healing, is under utilized in times of crisis. Imasogie pleas for an embodiment of the gospel in distinctly African ways.

All of the voices we have heard move toward a synthetic model for contextual theology. The examples cited from O. M. Rao and Osadolor Imasogie are representative.

A praxis model of contextual theology also undergirds each of the accents we have heard, but this model is best seen in the essay by Eddie Kin-ming Ma from Hong Kong.[7] The political climate of Hong Kong, facing reabsorption into China, helps shape the relevance of the gospel for Hong Kong. There is no doubt that the culture of Hong Kong is going to change, and change quickly, in the near future. What is in doubt is whether or not the gospel will have significant influence in the midst of radical change. A praxis model for contextual theology concedes that change is imminent and, therefore, invests itself toward become an authentic agent of change in light of the gospel. Kin-ming Ma's careful description of a gospel that strives toward covenant, community, and the kingdom is helpful for all who find themselves in the midst of rapid change. His closing words, which reflect the distinctives of a praxis model of theology, also are a prayer for the work of the gospel:

> My prayer is not only writing about contextualization but really putting it into practice in my own church, among my own people, in my own land, so that the Hong Kong Chinese may fully understand what the Gospel means to them.[8]

UNCOMMON THEMES

In addition to the common themes of gratitude for missionary efforts in the South, tempered with concerns for the cultural captivity of the gospel preached and lived by the missionaries, and the common examples of contextual theology that conforms to synthetic and praxis models,[9] some uncommon themes emerged in varying accents, as well. "Uncommon" refers both to the fact that a majority of presenters did not sound one of the following themes, and the perception that the following themes will seem unusual to readers from the West and North.

The Challenge of Community

Six of the accents we have heard stressed the importance of community in their contexts. Douglas Waruta and Osadolor Imasogie (Africa), Wati Aier and O. M. Rao (Asia), Eddie Kin-ming Ma (Southeast Asia), and Guillermo Catalán (Latin America) each held up the ideal of community as a central aspect of the health of theology in their contexts. Of course an emphasis upon community should not be an uncommon emphasis for Christian theology in any context; what makes the emphasis uncommon coming from Africa, Asia, Southeast Asia, and Latin America is what the emphasis intends to argue against.

O. M. Rao succinctly expressed the theme: "Western individualism—including the idea that beliefs are personal and do not change one's participation in the larger community—created difficulties for converts to Christianity."[10] Individualism, some would add the adjective "radical," is so much a part of the worlds of the North and West that a challenge to the personal and individual dimension of the gospel as proclaimed and lived is uncommon, indeed. Waruta, Imasogie, Aier, Rao, Kin–ming Ma, and Catalán do not intend to diminish the demand that each person have a significant encounter with Christ. Not at all! Their clear evangelical bearings would not allow anything but a theology of personal transformation that comes through an experience with Christ Jesus. What they do stress, however, is that it is the community of believers that, as a whole, carries the light of the gospel in their cultural contexts.

A Willingness for Dialogue

Six of the accents we have heard also expressed a willingness to enter dialogue with individuals and groups representing other religions. Harrison Olan'g (Africa), Wati Aier and O. M. Rao (Asia), Ken Manley and Brian Smith (Southeast Asia), and Guillermo Catalán (Latin America) each framed the context of the gospel in their worlds against the backgrounds of traditional regional religions (Olan'g and Manley), global religions such as Hinduism and Islam (Aier and Rao), manifestations of a secular faith (Smith), and even the imposing reality of the Roman Catholic Church as a cultural force (Catalán).

The confessions of responsibility and hope of Wati Aier clarify the uncommon theme of willingness to enter dialogue with others:

> Our goal as Asian Christians is to awaken faith under the Lordship of Christ. In the dialogue with other religions, we do not lose our identity, but have the possibility of emerging from the dialogues with new profiles. It may be said that these profiles will be turned towards abolition of prejudices about other faiths, and be passionate about others suffering and justice and their future, towards full life in Christ.[11]

The uncommonness of this theme can be traced to its openness to dialogue with faiths, even secular ones, which compete for attention with the gospel. Perhaps it is because some of the accents that have sounded a willingness to dialogue have in common with other faiths a minority status, or perhaps it is because those accents also confess a confidence in the power of the gospel to interpret itself (see Catalán's closing anecdote[12]). Whatever the reason, a willingness to enter dialogue with people who hold faith claims rooted in traditions other than Baptist is uncommon, indeed.

Principles for Enrichment

We conclude our report on what we have heard with seven principles for enrichment that we have extrapolated from the papers presented at the conference. As is the case with all principles, the seven we note have been shaped cumulatively by the conference participants.

1. The task of interpretation is always contextual and situational. Therefore, theological pursuits in general and biblical interpretation in particular demand that theologians spend ample time and energy exploring the contexts and situations that demand the insights of an interpreter.

2. An understanding of the biblical message is not merely a psychological disclosure of the mind of the interpreter, or even a translation of the changeless biblical message into the vernacular, changing understanding of the interpreter. Understanding the biblical message requires both a reading and rereading of a given text in the context of the world, perspectives, and categories of a particular interpreter (or interpreters) and the intended audience.

3. Eisegesis (reading into) and exegesis (reading out of) are two poles of the same equation. Interpreters must not see their subjectivity—which leads to eisegesis—necessarily as a negative limitation as they strive to understand a text. Focusing attention on the subjectivity that produces eisegesis can become an avenue for awareness that, in turn, becomes a positive perspectival advantage for the tasks of authentic interpretation sought through exegesis.

4. Third-World theologies do not approach the Bible necessarily according to First-World hermeneutics, mainly the historical-critical method. Because the Third-World has not embraced the worlds and insights of modern science, Third-World theologies tend to be more intuitive than critical. At the same time, because a significant number of Third-World theologians and teachers were trained in First-World settings, they usually know First-World perspectives better than First-World theologians know Third-World perspectives. When Third-World interpreters of the gospel choose not to employ First-World methods the choice is neither a sign of weakness or lack of training.

5. Third-World interpretations of the gospel are principally communal and practical. They depend more on the interpretations of

a particular community and its needs, usually a local church, than upon the conclusions of scholarly research and theories that appear unrelated to the life of the community at worship and work.

6. Third-World hermeneutics tend to follow in the path of a strong theologian who is well known in the region, but who may not be known outside a given geographical area. In other cases, theologians are merely compilers of popular Christian theologies, usually mixed with popular religiosity. Both approaches and themes must be observed and considered carefully.

7. Theologies from the periphery that have gained attention in the worlds of the North and West often have been popularized by theologians of the North and West. The popularizing often includes either adding or subtracting essential elements of those theologies from the periphery simply because the elements are not considered important for northern and western readers. In such instances, Third-World theologies have suffered in silence misinterpretations and distorted characterizations. Therefore, it is better to have a Third-World theologian interpret his or her understanding of the gospel.

What we have heard is that the gospel grows richer, broader, and deeper when spoken with a variety of accents. What we hope to hear in the future is more conversation about what is most important to our lives as Christian theologians. We hope to hear the gospel proclaimed and interpreter in as many accents as there are cultures and languages.

NOTES

[1]Daniel Carro explores the relativity of "the ends of the earth" and the beginning of the earth in the final essay in this book.

[2]Stephan B. Bevans, *Models of Contextual Theology* (Maryknoll, New York: Orbis Books, 1992). See Richard F. Wilson's introductory essay, "Contextual Theology and Global Baptists," which explores Bevans's work as a way to identify the diversity of theology as pursued in contemporary settings. By employing Bevans's models we do not intend to "pigeonhole" and thereby restrict any of the accents we have heard. The models are tools that may help us, and our readers,

glimpse some of the distinctives of the variety of contextual theologies that are being pursued in the South.

[3]See Wilson, "Contextual Theology," (7), and Bevans, 30–46.

[4]See Wilson, "Contextual Theology," (8–9), and Bevans, 81–96, and 63–80.

[5]See O. M. Rao, "An Indian Gospel for India," (63–69).

[6]See Osadolor Imasogie, "A Gospel for Nigerians," (40–47).

[7]See Eddie Kin-ming Ma, "A Gospel of Covenant, Community, and Kingdom," (77–81).

[8]Ibid., (81).

[9]The careful reader may wonder whether we have forgotten the models of contextual theology that Bevans characterizes as "anthropological" and "transcendental" (see Wilson, "Contextual Theology," 7, 9, and Bevans, 47–62 and 97–110). Those models, while clearly present in the broad theological picture Bevans describes, do not lend themselves to the doing of theology that is characteristic of global Baptists. The sharp focus upon scripture that Baptists bring to the tasks of theology seems to prevent them from placing either culture or experience (the emphases of anthropological and transcendental theologies, respectively) on an equal plane with biblical understandings of revelation.

In another exploration it might be interesting and helpful to search for examples of Baptist theology that approach anthropological and transcendental contextualizing. This study, however, is more interested in describing what we have heard.

[10]See O. M. Rao, "An Indian Gospel for India," (64).

[11]See Wati Aier, "A Gospel of Christ, *Not* Christianity," (61).

[12]See Guillermo Catalán, "A Gospel Lived," (108–109).

Reflections on Culture
and the Understanding of the Gospel

Daniel Carro

"Go therefore and make disciples of all nations" (Matt 28.19). "Go into all the world and preach the gospel to the whole creation" (Mark 16.15). "You shall be my witnesses...to the end of the earth" (Acts 1:8). The echoes of the missionary mandate of our Lord still resound with their original power: Pervade, with the holy influence of the gospel, to the end of the earth, to the whole of creation, to all peoples, to all cultures, to the whole society.

How to fulfill both the demands of the mandate, including when, where, and under what circumstances the gospel is to be preached, and how to address the problems that arise from differing understandings of the gospel and its praxis, contribute to the complexity of twenty centuries of Christian history. Because every understanding of the gospel is culturally bound, and because every expression of faith and every theology is wrapped in the cocoons of culture, the variety of expressions that the gospel has taken through the years is impossible to quantify.

When contemporary Christians reflect upon culture and the understanding of the gospel we need to do so primarily with the goal of clarifying the matter for our day, and in the context of our diverse world. Our goal should go beyond the production of papers and books and toward the identification of some valuable tools we could use to foster both the understanding and the praxis of the mission of the church as we approach the twenty–first century.

Culture and Society

At the beginning of these reflections, let us point to a common misunderstanding between two related concepts: culture and society. These terms and concepts are not synonymous; each has a particular meaning and focus. Culture is the medium, the broad context, in which society is formed, while society is product of culture. Culture is the mix of values and expressions found in a particular place, while society is what emerges when the mix of values and expressions is sorted and sifted according to priorities (which is why a single culture may provide a home for multiple societies). Culture tends toward change, while society tends toward stability.

The clearest popular definition of society I have heard recently came from a former drug addict, now afflicted with AIDS, during an interview shown on television. He said: "Society is everybody, except me." The notion is clear whether we agree with him or not. Society is in the business of establishing priorities of acceptance and rejection. Those who fall outside of the accepted limits experience society as cruel and cold. For the person in the interview, society was everybody except him. For those on the "outside" society is incomprehensible, a source of judgement and condemnation.

Too often Christians have merely followed the prevailing patterns of understanding culture and society rather than challenging them with the truths of the gospel. As a result we have helped build the kinds of walls that make the sick, the unattractive, the poor, the minorities feel and think that "society is everybody, except me." There should be another way of thinking and believing.

A Christian Understanding of Culture and Society

A Christian understanding of culture and society should be illuminated by the light of revelation, specifically the revelation of God in Christ and the subsequent rise of the church as the Body of Christ. In the fine light of revelation Christians confess that culture and society are communitarian realities. The Godhead is communal—how else could trinitarian confessions be interpreted?—and the broad context of the world is a reflection of divine communal nature. Culture itself is formed in the making of that communion. Humankind is always in communio with God, with others, and with the self. The basic communion of God with God also provides insights into the communal foundation for culture, and for society.

There is society because humankind is communal, as is God. For Christians, society takes shape in communities because culture is communitarianly formed as a reflection of the work of God as creator. The society shaped by revelation, the church as the Body of Christ, is not against the culture from which it springs, but is, instead, a continuing reflection of God as redeemer and sustainer in the world.

In light of revelation Christians should see society and culture integrationally. Integration is a social union or synthesis in which human assimilation is made possible by desegregation, by breaking down barriers that separate. The Body of Christ is the perfect integrative society: "There is neither Jew nor Greek, there is neither slave nor free, there is neither male nor female; for you are all one in Christ Jesus" (Gal 3.28). All Christians are children of God, all have been baptized in the same baptism, all are inheritors of God's promises given to Abraham and Sarah. When a culture is influenced by the authentic Body of Christ in its midst, the possibility of integration is enhanced. When a society receives Christian discipleship, integration is more likely to become a reality.

A Christian society is *oikoumene* (*oikos*, meaning "house," and *menos*, meaning "dwelling"), a place where humankind can dwell in communion with God. *Oikoumene* is the world, but only in the sense of a world inhabited by human beings. The *oikoumene* is the place we humans occupy, where we make our mores, which are not merely our morals, but also the character upon which they rest and from which they derive meaning. When culture is *oikoumen*ically influenced, human character derives more nearly according to divine patterns. When a society has been formed according to a communal understanding of the world, a divine shape takes form in it. The more communally culture is formed, the more divine society results.

Our Past Definitions of Culture and the Gospel

In the past, Christian definitions of the cultural implications of the gospel have tended to be too scientific, too Eurocentric, and influenced too often by values and expressions outside the light of revelation. We have tended to be too scientific in arenas where scientific criteria have not been established as credible or valid. To preach the gospel to "all nations" means more than keeping a "scientific" record of how many nations have become home to missionaries. "The end of the earth" definitely is not the "scientific" missionary city of Ushuaia, the city farthest south in the Argentine Patagonia.

All nations (or all peoples) are never reached, because new "nations," are being formed every day over the face of the earth, enlarging the *oikoumene*. Furthermore, the "end" of the earth depends on where one begins geographically and culturally. It was natural for the English missionary Allen Gardiner, in 1851, to consider that he had reached "the end of the earth: Ushuaia." Had the missionary been from the Patagonia of Argentina, the end of the earth perhaps would be more properly called England!

Secondly, we have tended to be too Eurocentric in our vision of the world. That seems natural to us who, in one way or another, proceed from Europe. But a vision of culture that is too Eurocentric ignores, if not denies, other cultures and other societies. Those who are different from the European ideals remain out of our scope of comprehension, unreached by "our" kind of gospel.

Christianity was never intended to be an Eurocentric faith. The early church, as we can read about in Acts 10–11, had to learn painfully that an ethnic gospel was an impediment to God's will. The gospel was not to be considered a property of the Jews in the first century, and it is not today a property of the European. Neither will the gospel be confined by White, Black, Yellow, Indian, Hispanic, or any other center. "For what we preach is not ourselves, but Jesus Christ as Lord, with ourselves as your servants for Jesus' sake," said Paul (2 Cor 4.5).

Christianity, it would seem, has become captive of a Eurocentric culture, which now, at the end of the twentieth century, is being proposed as the culture of the world. But to maintain its proper nature, the Body of Christ must not be deceived by its Eurocentrism. Instead we must enter into a dialogue with other cultures, trying to become a foundational part of any of the non-Eurocentric cultures that populate the world. To do less is to turn our back on the missionary mandate of our Lord.

Moreover, we have tended to be too adaptive in our understanding of culture and the gospel. We have assumed that there is one model of culture and one model of the gospel for every society. Therefore, with the one-size-fits-all mentality, we thought we only have to adapt that "model" culture and that "model" gospel to the imperfect, finite and corrupt cultures and societies where all the world lives every day.[1]

We know that the ideal Body of Christ does not exist. Neither church nor society has achieved maturity. The perfect church or society is a hope, an educational pattern that does not really exist, yet. The church "in splendor, without spot or wrinkle or any such thing...holy and without blemish," that Paul describes to the Ephesians (6.27) only exists as an eschatological hope. Thus we are reminded that the Christian community was never intended to be an adaptation of adaptations of adaptations through the centuries of an unique, ideal and typical model.

On the contrary, vital Christian faith has always been rooted and has grown in every society by its own means. Christian faith, as any other social product of human culture has had to fight itself and the circumstances of its existence in order to shape what has been produced. A Christian society, and the larger culture which it has borne witness to have grown mainly ex abruptum.

So, if we want gain a way through which perhaps we can find a valuable answer for the problem of the relation of culture, society, and the gospel, we must first abandon our scientific, Eurocentric and adaptive pretensions, and gain a new and more humble point of view, rooted in revelation, over the gospel and society.

A New Point of View on Culture, Society, and the Gospel

In order to gain a new point of view on culture, society, and the gospel, we need to treat all interpretive proposals as provisional and investigate the social background of the proponent with the purpose to make ourselves more conscious of our own particular ethnocentrisms and provincialisms.

Everybody seems to agree that "the early bird gets the worm," but what does the proverb mean for the early worm? We need to acknowledge there are always two sides to every coin. Latin Americans (who also are Americans) have been called the "the other side of the coin," "the under-side of history," or the "backyard."

We have to ask ourselves, what it should look like to construct theology from the backyard, what reflections on God and humanity could come from the underside of history, and how is the Christian faith to be seen from the other side of the coin?

Robert McAfee Brown, noted North American theologian who has joined conversations with theologians in places other than the privileged North and West, made five fine reflections on biblical interpretation based on observations he made in my city, Buenos Aires: (1) What one sees in a biblical text is not necessarily what is there, (2) What one sees depends on where one is standing, (3) When others tell what they see, the hearers needs to know where they are standing as well as where the speaker stands, (4) No matter how much anybody sees, nobody sees it all, and (5) What is seen is always subject to correction.[2]

Brown made his reflections with reference to the reading and interpretation of biblical texts. His comments are also very good as points of departure toward the interpretation of cultural texts and contexts. The following builds on Brown's cautions for biblical interpreters and expands them for those interested in interpreting cultural and social contexts.

What One Sees Is Not Necessarily What Is There

Interpretation is a concealed act carried out, at least initially without thinking and without reflection. It is instantaneous, impulsive, automatic, unconscious, spontaneous, instinctive, and involuntary. Between the interpreter and the interpreted thing there is what has been called a "hermeneutic circle."[3] The "circle" has two phases. The first phase develops when all the understanding of the interpreter is applied to the object under consideration. An interpreter always brings preconceptions to that which is interpreted. The second phase transpires when all the reality of the object of interpretation strikes the mind of the interpreter with its hardness and rigidity. The interplay between the subject (the interpreter) and the object (that which is to be interpreted) makes it possible to speak of a preunderstanding (*a priori*) and postunderstanding (*a posteriori*). Interpretation begins with the preunderstanding.

The interpretive structure described in the previous paragraph is also present when interpreters focus attention on a culture, whether the interpreter has been born into it or whether the interpreter is a stranger. The interpretation of a culture does not differ in any way from any other type of interpretation. What a certain interpreter may see in a culture is not necessarily what is there. Preunderstandings of the culture may blind the one born into it, or they may obscure the perception of the one who is a strange. Neither one of the perspectives is better than the other; both are needed. The inside-out vision of the interpreter does not necessarily supersede or abolish the outside-in vision, or vice versa.

There is no bias-free interpretation. Having confessed that truth, interpreters no longer need to look for such a creature. Instead of trying to avoid a biased interpretation (which cannot be done), the interpreter must find a place in the hermeneutic circle and begin to circulate. The more the circle turns, the better chance the interpreter has to understand the object of interpretation.

What One See Depends on Where One Stands

The term "world" also can be understood as a "world of significance." Both the literal and figurative use of the term evokes an understanding of a 'horizon" that frames the world. The horizon also determines what may be excluded or included in a given world. In the literal world, for example, the night sky in the southern and northern hemispheres are quite different: in the North there is no Southern Cross; in the South there is no Big Dipper. The horizons of a figurative world can be illustrated thorough a walk with the family around a shopping mall: each member of the family will be drawn to store windows and displays that come closest to matching his or her interests.

The reality of horizons and worlds has been described by philosophers as "perspectivism." The Spanish philosopher José Ortega y Gassett describes perspectivism: "Cosmic reality is such that it only can be seen under one determined perspective. Perspective is one of the components of reality. Far from being its deformation, it is its organization."[4]

Perspectivism is not a loss, but a gain. The main point of perspectivism is that each person possess a valuable point of view of the whole. Every person has a unique vision of the whole and, therefore, every viewpoint is irreplaceable in the pursuit of wholeness. The whole is only gained through a combination of all perspectives. Each person assists in shaping the whole by the vital integration that she or he makes in life. The integration is not made in an artificial or ideal construction that is produced in the mind of an intellectual, but in a particular living out of the consequences of the given interpretation.

Ortega y Gassett continues, "An abstract point of view only produces more abstractions," and, therefore

> The species aeternitates of Spinoza, that ubiquitous and absolute point of view, does not exist properly. It is fictitious and abstract. We do not doubt its instrumental utility for certain needs of knowledge, but it is necessary not to forget that from it reality is not to be seen. Reality, as a landscape, has infinite perspectives, all of them equally true and authentic. The only false perspective is that one that pretends to be unique. In other words: false is utopia, truth not localized, as seen from nowhere.[5]

We must not fear the distortions we experience when we try to see the whole from the part, or when we attempt to visualize the world from our own personal, individual, partial, perspectives. The only thing we should fear is to have those beautiful, exemplary, great opinions that neither affect nor reflect reality at all because they are too utopian, too disembodied, or too ideal.

The ideal of an "objective" interpretation depends on a scientific world-view. But the majority of people in the Third World have not been introduced to science. They have a different world-view. They interpret things differently, including culture and the gospel.

Both Speaker and Hearer Should Know Where They Stand

One point provides perspective; two points indicate direction; three points allow for depth. No interpreter is able to trace a perspective until the perspectives of others have been examined, if not explored. Everyone needs to be aware and open to other points of view of culture, whether it is the culture of one's home or not.

In the contemporary setting who asks Third World people their perspectives? Who cares about the points of view of people who have been rendered faceless and voiceless by the economic, political, and intellectual "centers" of the First World? More pointed for our reflections on culture and the understanding of the gospel, if the church refuses to hear and explore the perspectives of Third World Christians, then the Body of Christ will be deprived. The church will lose a chance to plumb the depths of understanding the gospel made possible through the confessions and constructions of believers who stand outside the First World.

When a person interprets a culture, the interpretation moves at least two ways. The first movement is from the interpreter toward others, and the second movement is the receiving of the others as partners in the interpretation. Interpreting a given culture involves interpreting lives, communities, hopes, and fears. The twin movements cannot be avoided, and neither can they be planned. As has been stated above, the act of interpretation is not pursued or avoided, rather it is unconscious.

The *locus theologicus* from which any person envisions theology is important and should remain open to dialogue with those from other loci. No one person has possession of the perfect *locus theologicus*. Every *locus* is merely a *locus*. All cultural interpretations of the nature of the gospel are equally valid. As disturbing as it may seem to some, the viewpoints of others, especially those from other cultures, are as valid as one's own. From the recognized economic, political, and intellectual "centers" of the First World, such a claim must appear as a scandal.

"Central" theologies, exported to the rest of the world with their cultural trappings, should now be reinterpreted by the same "central" theologians in light of their encounters with other cultures and perspectives. To do less jeopardizes both the direction and depth of the gospel in the contemporary world.

Nobody Sees It All

There is no perfect interpretation. A learned interpretation is not automatically better than and unlearned one. For instance, in the practice of biblical interpretation a more precise reading, according to established historical-critical methods, does not mean necessarily a better reading. Recent developments in "postmodernism" demonstrate that the historical-critical paradigm for theological scholarship is being called into question as the way to approach the biblical literature.

As Paul Ricouer has argued, the historical-critical method pursed by learned scholars may succeed in getting "behind" the biblical texts, but the forward looking approach to the texts is often accomplished by the unlearned who invest themselves in applying the texts to concrete circumstance. Some interpretations are better in the "behind" mode, while others are better in the "ahead" mode. The learned interpreter is generally better in the searching behind the text, and the unlearned interpreter seems to be better in anticipating where the text leads the contemporary reader and community.

Between the "behind" and the "ahead" readings there is the reminder that no one interpreter of the text—and by implication, no one interpreter of the cultures in which texts are read and discussed—sees it all. Every interpreter needs other interpreters to focus direction and fill in the depth of meaning that comes from texts and cultures.

What Is Seen Is Always Subject to Correction

Turning again to Robert McAfee Brown, "the application of [the above] insights...should also verge on the self-evident."[6] If interpretation of texts and cultures requires multiple perspectives and an openness to the insights of those who live and breathe in different cultural contexts, then it follows that every interpretation should anticipate, if not expect, corrective suggestions from other points of view. A sober reflection upon culture and the meaning of the gospel should include a willingness to ponder every attempt to correct each effort to proclaim the gospel in a world marked by diversity.

Culture, Society and the Nature of the Gospel

Culture, society, and the gospel as interpreted in context form a kind of triangle, a hermeneutic triangle. The contemporary gospel accents heard in the heart of this book provide excellent examples of how the broad context of culture—African, Asian, Southeast Asian, and Latin American—is the soil from which societies of the gospel spring. In each case above the writers acknowledge the dominant culture from which they speak, and they confess the deep hopes of the church (a society, as defined at the beginning of this essay) in that context. Taking seriously both cultural contexts and societal hopes for stability, the writers have offered fresh interpretations of the gospel. Taken singularly, each confession illuminates one way of experiencing the power of the gospel. Taken as a whole, these confessions add depth to the meaning of the gospel for all who live in its light.

"Culture," "society," and "gospel" are fluid concepts that require reinterpretation each time they are used and encountered. As a result, they can be difficult realities to grasp, especially if approached from limited and rigid perspectives. To gain a valuable perspective on all three, we must first abandon our categories of superiority that claim to be all-inclusive and comprehensive. Abandoning inadequate and partial perspectives does not mean the loss of a sure foundation, however. Being open to the possibility that another point of view on the gospel rooted in a different culture and society is a first step toward recognizing that the foundation of the gospel does not exclusively rest with those who confess it and interpret it. Recall Paul's words to the Corinthians that he and Apollos were cooperative workers as they interpreted the gospel out of their own experiences (1 Cor 3.1-9). Recall the image of the Letter to the Hebrews that makes distinctions between the "builder of the house" and the one who serves in it (Heb 3.1-6).

The mission of the church, a society of the gospel that emerges in diverse cultures, is not compromised in the venture of reinterpreting the gospel and our theologies in context. What comes of the task is broadening and deepening of our understanding of gospel. A more clear understanding of the gospel may challenge our superior notions that one interpretation of the gospel (usually understood as "my" interpretation) should prevail. In that way every interpretation is open to challenge. But the gospel itself will not be challenged! Instead, a gospel more broadly and deeply understood will challenge every interpretation in every context.

We need an open reading of the nature of the gospel in a given culture that will also foster openness in every other context. We need an authentically communal interpretation of the nature of the gospel that is willing to be embraced by the confessions of the Apostles' Creed: "I believe in the communion of saints," and "I believe in the holy catholic church." The church cannot be confined to a hemisphere or a continent. There no such thing as the church of the South or the church of the North. There is one church, one body, one faith, one baptism. In the church all belong to all. And the same may be said for our interpretations of the gospel.

NOTES

[1]See Richard F. Wilson's essay, "Contextual Theology and Global Baptists" for an illustration of how multiple models of contextual theology may be explored.

[2]Robert McAfee Brown, *Theology in a New Key* (Philadelphia: Westminster Press, 1978), especially chapter 3, "The Melodic Stridency of Scripture," 75–100.

[3]The idea of a hermeneutic circle is best explored by Juan Luís Segundo, *The Liberation of Theology* (Maryknoll, New York: Orbis Books, 1976). Brown, and nearly every other interpreter of cross-cultural hermeneutics, draws significant insight from Segundo's analysis.

[4]José Ortega y Gassett, *El Tema de Nuestro Tiempo* (Madrid: Rev. de Occidente, 1970 [1923 original publication]), 105, author translation.

[5]Ibid., 105–107.
[6]Brown, 85.

Contributors

Wati Aier is a Professor at the Oriental Theological Seminary in Madras, India.

Daniel Carro is a Professor of Greek, Hermeneutics, and Philosophy at the International Baptist Theological Seminary in Buenos Aires, Argentina.

Guillermo I. Catalán is President and a Professor at the Chilean Baptist Theological Seminary in Santiago, Chile.

L. A. (Tony) Cupit is the Director of the Evangelism and Education Division of the Baptist World Alliance, headquartered in McLean, Virginia, United States.

Rolando Gutiérrez-Cortés is a Pastor in Colonia Prado, Mexico.

Osadolor Imasogie is the Principal of the Nigerian Baptist Seminary in Benin City, Nigeria.

Renthy Kreitzer is a Professor at Eastern Theological Seminary in Assam, India.

Louise Kretzschmar is Professor in the Department of Systematic Theology at the University of South Africa in Pretoria, South Africa.

Eddie Kin-ming Ma is a Professor at the Hong Kong Baptist Theolgoical Seminary in Hong Kong.

Ken Manley is a Professor at Whitley College, University of Melbourne, Pikeville, Victoria, Australia.

Billy Mathias is a Pastor in Bandung, West Java, Indonesia.

Harrison G. Olan'g is a Professor at International Baptist Theological Seminary of Eastern Africa in Tanzania.

O. M. Rao is a Professor at the Carey Centre in Calcutta, India.

Carlos Villanueva is a Professor of Old Testament at the International Baptist Theological Seminary in Buenos Aires, Argentina.

Douglas Waruta is a Professor at National University in Nairobi, Kenya.

Richard F. Wilson is a Professor in The Roberts Department of Christianity, College of Liberal Arts, at Mercer University in Macon, Georgia, United States.